Grief and Grace

Stories at the Intersection of Life and Death

Text and Photos by

Cynthia Greb

This is an expanded second edition of
Grief and Grace: Essays on Love and Beauty in the Midst of Dying.
The first edition was published in December 2018.
This second edition was published in August 2019.

Table of Contents

Foreword

One crisp Sunday afternoon when the air beckoned me to the country, I ventured out to a gathering at an interfaith church in Bucks County, Pennsylvania. The program facilitator invited us to form two circles, one inside the other, the outer circle facing inward and the inner circle facing outward. We were asked to remain silent and offer a greeting through our eyes to each person as the circles turned in opposite directions. That is how I met Cindy. I remember because as we looked at each other, we both had a deep knowing that we already "knew" one another, even though we had never met. We became easy friends, eventually sharing many interests, spiritual study circles, women's groups and, after several years of study, ordination as interfaith ministers. What our minds had not understood on that Sunday, our hearts clearly did. We were sister hospice chaplains in the making.

In *Grief and Grace*, Cynthia has created the perfect soothing companion for committed but weary caregivers to the dying and those navigating the unpredictable journey of grief. Disclosing some of her own most difficult experiences, raw emotions and unexpected blessings, she bravely meets the reader in one of the most challenging intersections on life's roadmap. That is, the crossroad where loving and losing intersect, where knowledge is met with uncertainty, where control has been stolen by the wind and only love can lead the way.

As hospice professionals, we know that we don't "get a discount" when it is our turn to face the death of a loved one. As a caregiver or family member of the dying, all of our expertise leaves us grappling with the very same uncertainties and conflicting emotions that all families face.

At the same time, finding grace and beauty in the midst of death is not reserved for the hospice professional. That is the greatest gift of this book. Cynthia's moments of pause, connecting with nature, her God, and her heart reveal unexpected support and blessing.

May we learn from her to be willing, available, and open to those moments in each of our days.

Reverend Helen (Lady) Burke
Pastoral Counselor
Philadelphia, PA

Introduction

It is nearly impossible to escape life on this planet without experiencing the pain of loss. Unless one dies very young, each person is likely to experience the death of multiple loved ones during the course of a lifetime. Grief is such a universal experience.

Several years ago when I began the first of two jobs as a hospice chaplain, I was 50 years old. Interestingly, in spite of my age, at that time I was not intimately acquainted with death. My grandparents and a handful of other friends and acquaintances had died, but I hadn't been submerged in the grief that happens when one accompanies someone on his or her journey toward the end of life. Then in 2013, beginning with my father's rapid decline and, just two years later, my mother's and a whole host of others, all of my inexperience changed as I was bombarded by a string of deaths, back to back to back.

Dad's deterioration was the result of Alzheimer's coupled with a bad fall. I was with him for the last three months of his life and was so grateful to be with him when he took his last breath. Sixteen months later, my beautiful young niece died unexpectedly, only 19 years old. This caused the axis of the world to irrevocably shift for her parents and all who loved her. Then, after years of wobbly health, my mother also passed, only one month after my niece. As with Dad, I was blessed to be with her for the last three months of her life, and by grace, to be with her at her last breath. Meanwhile, while I was with my parents in Pennsylvania, two especially dear caregiving clients in Colorado passed away, and another client about a month after Mom. In addition, within this same approximate three-year period, three uncles and two former boyfriends died. Wham, wham, wham. Death had caught up with me and my loved ones, big time.

Someone who didn't believe so absolutely in an afterlife might have been shaken to the core. Although I certainly felt grief, as some of the following stories will show, I was mostly just exhausted. Caring for those you love in the last months or years of their lives is a marathon I would wish on no one.[1] And yet, as more and more baby boomers are caring for elderly parents, I know I have had lots of unfortunate company.[2]

This book is about both anticipatory grief and the mourning which occurs after a loved one dies. As I share the stories of caring for my parents and clients as they near the end of their lives, all the fatigue, stressors, and crazy soup of emotions are on full display. But sitting right alongside the challenging emotions are also all the tender and unexpected instances of grace and beauty. I noticed that many times, just when I was at the lowest of low points, something magical would happen to pull me back into a feeling of serenity and gratitude. During these exquisite instances of grace I would be reminded that life was so much more than an endless slogging through of one day after another. In the midst of exhaustion, grief, and despair, there was also great beauty and, most of all, love. In these moments of grace I would

---

[1] An article published by Senior Living.com states that, "Almost half of all baby boomers say tending to their own health and well-being comes second to caring for the health needs of loved ones."
https://www.seniorliving.com/article/baby-boomers-put-own-health-back-burner-care-parents

[2] The Family Caregiver Alliance reveals that in 2018, over 34 million Americans have provided unpaid care for elders over 50 years old. https://www.caregiver.org/caregiver-statistics-demographics

realize, without a doubt, that I was not alone; I was loved by Beings unseen.

When I was getting my ministerial training,[3] there was a plaque at the front of our primary classroom which I always loved. It is attributed to Desiderius Erasmus Roterodamus. It says, "Bidden or unbidden, God is present."

Yes, we are never alone.

Many of the following chapters are based on articles, essays, and blog posts I wrote during and after those years that were so full of loved ones dying, especially my dear parents. But several, such as the one about saying goodbye to my mother, were freshly written. The tears flowed once again though three years had passed.

Rather than organize these essays and stories in strict chronological order, I have arranged them in a progression from 1) times of caregiving, to 2) the time when death is near, to 3) the special graces that can happen after our loved ones die. Each chapter will be dated for your reference. At the suggestion of a friend, I also included some blank pages in the back on which readers can record the thoughts and feelings which arise over the course of reading this book.

The topic of dying, death, and the afterlife is a huge one, but this particular book is not meant to be comprehensive. When people are in the throes of grief or despair, they generally don't have the energy to

---

[3] The School of Sacred Ministries, Doylestown, Pennsylvania; https://schoolofsacredministries.org

read lengthy tomes. Sometimes, though, a few stories of inspiration can be just what the doctor ordered.

My prayer is that if you are one of the many caring for an ill or elderly loved one, in reading these stories you will feel less alone. I hope this book will bring you a modicum of comfort and peace; that it will help to lift the collective fear of death; and most especially that it will bring you closer to God, or Whomever or whatever you call that great loving and eternal Presence we are sometimes blessed, through sheer grace, to experience firsthand.

As one who has been there, I send you deep blessings. May you be touched by divine grace as you weave your way through some sad and challenging times.

Peace be with you.
Cynthia

Part I

CARING FOR LOVED ONES AS THEY NEAR THE END

When Someone You Love is Ill or Dying[4]

December 2013

When someone you love is very ill or dying, life has a way of shrinking. You may find yourself pulling back from the rest of the world as you shift your focus from your own affairs to this person whom you dearly love. Suddenly your world becomes you and your loved one and whoever else interacts with the two of you; and that's it.

You may find yourself losing interest in anything non-essential. You may find yourself unable to muster the energy to hang out with friends. Anything noisy chaotic or busy may feel too overwhelming. Like your loved one, you may find you need to focus inward.

You may find yourself postponing projects and canceling engagements. You may find yourself not caring about monetary affairs, not caring about your own health, and not caring about anyone else's concerns, valid though they may be.

---

[4] http://www.beliefnet.com/columnists/blessingsabound/2013/12/when-someone-you-love-is-ill-or-dying.html

You may find yourself sad and lethargic. You may find yourself quiet. You may find yourself sitting in a chair with no impulse to move anywhere.

All of this is normal in such a situation. You are wrestling with some big emotions--worry and fear, sadness and grief, compassion and love.

This is a time for great gentleness. This is not the time for self-judgment or shame. You are in one of the great existential periods of your life. You may find yourself asking "why" questions and coming up with no easy answers. Or perhaps your head understands a bit about what is going on but your heart is struggling nevertheless. This is hard work. Being ill and dying is very hard work. And loving the person who is ill or dying is hard work. Therefore, please be exceedingly kind to yourself. This is a tender and fragile time.

So what do you do when someone you love is very ill or dying? You love them to the best of your ability. And remember to love yourself as well.

Ask for help when it's needed. Ask for support from those able to give it. Seek comfort and guidance from your God and angels, if you believe in them. And please, don't do too much. Spend time in solitude. And if some healthy distraction is needed, allow yourself to succumb. Being a witness, a presence, and a support to someone struggling through an illness or death can be a marathon. And sometimes you may simply need a break. Allow it.

Grace[5]

December 2013

Last night I went to bed early, not because I was physically tired, but because I was emotionally worn out. I didn't have energy for anything other than the oblivion of a warm bed. But I did not sleep soundly as I had the previous several nights. Instead I was restless, thinking often of my father who was in the slow process of dying.

Eventually I gave up all notions of sleep and finally acknowledged the sadness that pervaded my being. I wasn't feeling distraught so much about his imminent passing, though I knew that would be hard; I was worried about his level of physical and emotional comfort. He was in a nursing home now and I was struggling to accept the situation. I couldn't be there every moment of every day making sure he was adequately cared for. And so I was awake, worrying.

Eventually I arose, got dressed, wrapped a blanket around me, and sat in a chair. At some point while sitting there I got the inspiration to take a walk outside. In the summer, this would have been an easier task, but in the winter it involved putting on several layers of clothing and deciding where I it was possible to

[5] http://www.beliefnet.com/columnists/blessingsabound/2013/12/grace.html

walk. The land was still coated with snow and ice from the most recent winter storm, and was likely to be slippery. Having traveled in warmer weather from Colorado to the family home in Pennsylvania, I had not brought boots with me. I decided to venture forth anyway.

I was surprised to find it snowing. I had heard something about the potential arrival of more snow, but listening to weather reports hadn't been high on my list of priorities recently. I looked at the tiny falling snowflakes lit by the streetlight at the end of our drive and felt a small shimmer of joy.

I set forth down the long crispy-crunchy driveway. I turned right to walk on the street that over the last forty years had become increasingly busy but at this time of night was blessedly quiet, as it had been during my childhood. I walked past two homes and turned into the parking lot of the elementary school I'd once attended. I no longer felt the need to walk. Instead I stopped under a lone streetlight and simply stood and gazed up at the sparkling flakes of falling snow.

I felt serenity steal over me. Alone in my room I had felt the weight of sorrow, but outside I was reminded that snow, like grace, falls on all of us--the well and the unwell, the caring and the indifferent, the human, the flora, and the fauna. We are each and all intricately connected.

I began to notice the sound of hundreds of brown crackled pin oak leaves, still attached to their mother tree and tap-tapping against one another in a small cool breeze. I heard the tiny comforting sound of hundreds of thousands of snowflakes landing upon those sweet leaves.

Grace. The beauty of the natural world was a balm to my spirit. Here it was, just outside the confines of the house I'd been trying to find shelter in. All I had to do was step outside.

I prayed that when I saw Dad in a few hours, I would be able to impart to him a bit of the serenity I was blessed to feel in these few precious moments.

I was feeling grateful. Grateful for all of it--the long process of dying, the serene beauty of the snow, life in all its myriad permutations. Simultaneously in our family's home lay my mother, married for fifty-six years to her beloved husband who was dying; a niece who was quietly anticipating the arrival of her first child; and another niece aglow with the love of a man she would be marrying in the new year. Life and death are all so intertwined. And the presence of death is what makes life all the more sweet.

Life is fleeting. May we savor it.

A Love Note from the Universe[6]

December 2013

One December day, in the midst of an emotionally exhausting time, I received a love note from the Universe.

This was the winter I was completely immersed in caring for my father. He was newly adjusting to being in a nursing home. We had kept him home as long as we possibly could, but his Alzheimer's was getting much worse. The caregivers, as well as each of my siblings and I, were struggling with the effort of caring for both parents while simultaneously taking care of a host of household duties that my parents were no longer capable of doing.

Dad was this wonderful, gregarious, laughing, loving man who had beautifully supported and loved a wife and five children. He was a lover of nature, had been a widely respected elder in two different churches, and was widely known for his teasing nature,

---

[6] This was first shared on the author's Facebook page. Later it was published in *Elephant Journal* as "Love Notes from the Universe."

his practical jokes, and his genuine love of life. And now he was rapidly losing his faculties.

I had been absolutely heartbroken that we had acquiesced to this nursing home solution. My one sister and I had been the holdouts. We wanted to keep Dad at home longer, however that option no longer seemed viable. Not only was he deteriorating more quickly each day, but the funds to pay for the 24-hour-a-day caregivers, as welll as all the other myriad expenses involved in maintaining my parents' large home, were disappearing fast. It seemed we had no choice.

There was a floor at this nursing home allocated for those with memory problems and those at risk of wandering. This was where Dad was living, in a room with three other men, two of whom called out relentlessly asking for help even when they'd just been checked on. It was good we had found a place where Dad would be safe. But I was also sad because he had regular periods of lucidity, and on this floor he was surrounded by what I know appeared to him to be "a bunch of crazies."

I hated for this proud and wonderful man to be there.

And so I spent time with him every day. I usually stayed for three to five hours at a time, then I tried to find time and energy for quality time with Mom who was still living in the family home. I was absolutely exhausted, never having enough time for my own needs, but I could not bear to *not* visit Dad, and Mom couldn't bear for me not to visit her.

One day, a couple weeks after he had moved in--in spite of an alarm which went off whenever he got up from his bed--Dad had found his way into the bathroom where, unsteady, he had fallen and hit his head.

After that, he went downhill fast. He could no longer walk on his own. He could no longer eat on his own. He started "checking out" by keeping his eyes closed even when he wasn't asleep. It was as if it had become too much effort to see. It was as if he no longer wanted to be a part of his environment.

We made the gut-wrenching decision to admit him to hospice care.

Now that he was even less capable of caring for himself or speaking up for himself, I came earlier and earlier in the day. I woke up worried about Dad. *Were they treating him right? Were they getting him to the bathroom when he needed to go? Were they giving him enough to drink? Was he comfortable?*

I began arriving around eight in the morning, sometimes even earlier. My immediate concerns were for his physical and emotional comfort. Oftentimes there was nothing for him to drink when he was thirsty (his drinks had to be thickened so he wouldn't choke) or he would have to go to the bathroom and no one would be responding to his calls. So I became the pesky daughter who would interrupt any passing aide or nurse politely asking for assistance.

One morning, my requests apparently became too much. The registered nurse in charge of the floor—an absolutely top notch nurse, very caring, respectful and professional—lost her temper with me. "What time is it, Cindy? What time is it?!" she demanded.

What she meant, I knew, was that it was still early in the day and each staff member had their hands full getting all the residents fed, washed, and dressed for the day.

I knew this. I knew this because I had once been one of them. When I was a teenager, I had been a nurse's aide in a nursing home. I knew firsthand how difficult the work was. I knew mornings were an especially busy time. I knew she was right. I knew I was there too early to begin my pestering. But at the same time I couldn't bear for my beloved father to be in discomfort.

Feeling chastised and unsure what to do, I fled. I hurried to the elevator, stumbled teary-eyed through the reception area, and practically ran down the front steps into the cold December air.

I started walking. I just started walking.

I walked for a couple blocks feeling a hundred emotions—sorrow, shame, despair, hopelessness, exhaustion, love. Everything tumbled around inside my heart. Tears slipped down my face as I walked, head hanging, on the shoveled sidewalks of town, past small piles of snow, large trees, parked cars.

Then I saw it. There at the edge of a sidewalk, all by itself, carved in melted ice, was a heart.

I stared at it incredulously. What were the chances? I knew it was the Universe telling me I was loved. In the midst of this massive love I felt for my father, in the midst of all my exhaustion, all my trying, all my human frailty, I was loved.

P.S. The next day I returned to see Dad. Of course I made sure to arrive no earlier than 9 a.m. I came prepared to apologize to Mary, the nurse. I knew how hard she worked. I knew how challenging the work was. I knew that every day she came and gave it her all. The last thing I wanted to do was make her job more difficult.

As I saw her and approached the desk, I opened my mouth to say how sorry I was. But she beat me to the punch. She, too, wanted to apologize. She quickly assured me, "You're a *wonderful* daughter. You're a *wonderful* daughter."

We both had tears in our eyes. It was clear that we understood we both had been doing the very best we could. How beautiful that we could come to a place of peace with one another.

Bless her and all nursing home staff everywhere. They work so very hard caring for the elders that we have difficulty caring for ourselves. They are, most certainly, earth angels.

Learning to Trust

December 2013

I finally figured out what I'm doing wrong. I figured out why I've been having so much trouble with Dad's move into the nursing home, with his recent decline, and with his current fevered state. It's not really that I'm afraid of him dying; it's that I don't want him to be uncomfortable. I don't want him to be uncomfortable emotionally, physically, or spiritually. I want to shield him from that. And that's too much for one person to do. In fact it's not possible for any one person to do. None of us has that kind of power. Not even a whole team of humans has that kind of power--because we're human and it's not within the scope of any human being.

I finally, finally got it. I haven't been able to completely place my trust in the staff of the nursing home because they are human. Even the compassionate, empathic, intuitive ones have bad days. Even the perceptive, knowledgeable, skilled nurses have limits. And certainly I can't be there 24 hours a day making sure everyone does everything exactly right every minute of the day. And that's what I've been trying to do: monitor Dad's every position, his every expression, looking for any nuance of pain or discomfort, constantly trying to assess whether or not he was okay. It was exhausting. No wonder I have dark circles under my eyes. I'm trying to do the impossible--protect someone from all possible harm.

I was lying in bed tonight, exhausted, sad, full of grief, feeling my love, my fears, my tears. I tried to imagine sending light and healing energy to the whole situation, but I wasn't feeling very successful. Then I had an epiphany. It finally occurred to me that I've been putting my faith in the wrong people. I've been putting my faith in *people!*

I realized that it was true that I couldn't completely trust the staff. After all, *I* was the one who noticed the fever; *I* noticed when they didn't have a pillow behind his head leaving his head tilted back and unsupported in a too-short chair; *I* noticed when he'd been fed too fast and food had been left, unswallowed and sitting in his mouth leaving him in danger of aspirating; *I* noticed when he was too hot or his feet were cold or there was something scratching his neck or cutting off the circulation in his arm. I knew the staff were not "bad" people. In fact most of them were *wonderful* people. But they were *people*, and thus fallible. So if I wasn't able to trust the staff, could I at least learn to trust Dad's guardian angel? Could I trust the Son of God whom my Dad so loved and honored? Could I trust God, the mighty Creator of the Universe? Surely these Holy Ones would take good care of my father if I could only learn to ask for Their help and then let go of control a little bit.

This was my big test. The only way I would ever achieve any measure of peace was if I could learn to trust that a heavenly team was not only hearing my prayers, but willing and eager to do as I asked – i.e., keep Dad comfortable and give him peace. I'd been forgetting to ask! I was so busy trying to be superhuman, that I forgot to pray for support from the heavenly support team. (Go, Heavenly Support Team!)

I'm not asking that Dad be kept alive indefinitely. I know there is divine wisdom in the cycle of life and death. I also know there is life after death. I'm not even asking that there be a miraculous cure to Alzheimer's or Parkinson's. All I want is for Dad to feel peace. And I think I can trust Them to do that.

So this is what I need to learn. I need to learn to trust the *non*-human realm (and maybe a few angels in human disguise). Once I learn this, *I* will find peace. And, come to think of it, that's the other important lesson. Can I allow *myself* to find peace?

Here is one more opportunity for me. In the face of both the kindness and capability I see *as well as* the fallibility, can I bless each nurse, aide, and administrator I see? Can I send blessings and love to the "good ones" and the kind ones *as well as* those who seem not quite as devoted or sensitive? Can I infuse the whole floor with love? And can I let them see my peace instead of my fear? Now *that* would be a very good thing.

Ahhh. So much to learn.

Beauty and Loss All Commingled[7]

October 26, 2015

Today I spent two hours with my ailing mother instead of the usual four to six. With the gift of an extra few hours in my day I decided to give myself the luxury of blessed time outside in sacred solitude. As I began to immerse myself in the silence and stillness of nature, I discovered myself sinking deeper into my "feeling body." Once again, I discovered that being too busy is anathema to the soulful existential questions and emotions I need to let bubble to the surface once in awhile.

Mom's health is declining. It hasn't been that stellar for quite a few years, but now her body is starting to fail in ways that are no longer remediable. I find myself wondering how conscious she is of her decline and when is the right time to discuss it all.

My mother has suffered from mood swings and a fair amount of depression these last several years. Even when she was living in her own home, surrounded by her loving (albeit increasingly demented) husband, excellent and compassionate caregivers, and

---

[7] Based on a blog post:
https://cindygreb.wordpress.com/2015/10/26/beauty-and-loss-all-commingl ed/

a regular rotation of visiting children and grandchildren, she frequently found reasons (not always easily discerned by us) to dissolve into tears. Being in a nursing home the last year and a half has certainly not resolved her feelings of depression.

Fortunately, when I recently asked the nurse on duty about the possibility of an antidepressant, she readily agreed that it would be wise and it was subsequently approved by the facility physician. I am not someone who ordinarily believes in indiscriminate pharmaceutical solutions, but her crying jags were disconcerting and I simply wanted her to feel better. (And, I should mention, Mom was in no way open to therapy.)

So the question of the hour is: do I open the can of worms that end-of-life discussions precipitate? Or shall I let her "feel good" for a little bit longer?

Unlike Dad, who embraced the idea of heaven and, though he loved life, looked forward to "going home," Mom only ever talked about death when she was unhappy with her life. For example, in a fit of self-pity she might say something like, "Well, I guess I might as well just die then." As you can imagine, I find myself hesitating to talk about something that could send her back into a downward spiral.

On the other hand, as someone who worked for two different hospices, I know how vitally important it is for those who are nearing death to have the opportunity to talk about these matters and to work through all the myriad emotions which will certainly arise.

And so, I pray for guidance to know when the time is right.

After leaving the nursing home earlier today and finishing a couple errands, I arrived home and dressed for that walk I'd promised myself. In the cool October air, I ambled down the path toward the stream at the bottom of the hill, I was struck by sights so achingly beautiful, I found myself invoking God's name in whispered awe over and over again.

The trees are aflame with color this year—golden yellows, vibrant oranges, beautiful corals and scarlets. Breathtaking and heart-opening beauty is everywhere. Even the skeletal remains of Queen Anne's lace and the dark petal-less heads of black-eyed Susans feel beautiful to me.

In addition to the splendors of autumn, there are lingering roses, hibiscus blooms, and purple clovers—splashes of summer in the midst of dying grasses and fallen leaves. Life and death are all commingled in this seasonal transition.

As I walked I found myself feeling the grief of Dad's absence in my life. Like me, he loved nature. We would have had some fine walks together this year had he still been alive. But I know we are both immersed in beauty and love—he where he is and I where I am. And Mom, too, though she is not as skilled at recognizing it or appreciating it. Then again, her childhood was not as special as Dad's or mine and my siblings'. When she was little she was given away by those who brought her into the world, and so abandonment is often her default emotional setting--even now, over seventy-five years later.

Beauty and Pain. Life and Death. Love and Loss. It's all here. We are surrounded by it all.

As my wise friend Kristy recently said, "Some things in life cannot be fixed. They can only be carried."

May I carry it all with grace.

The Next Season[8]

October 10, 2015

This is day #6 of being with parent #2 as she makes her slow exit from this world.

At the urging of my sister-in-law, I had flown home to be with Mom. She wasn't doing too well. Her heart rate had been in the 30's for days. Colette was a nurse and she was skilled at recognizing decline when she saw it. She wanted to make sure I knew how serious things were getting so that I could make the choice to be with Mom before it was too late. And so, heart in my mouth, I made arrangements to get home as soon as possible.

It's been an important and exhausting time. I am so grateful to be here with her, the woman who gave me birth. And, as anyone who has maintained a long vigil with someone who is very ill knows, it's a challenging road.

Today I had been feeling very low energy. I was extremely tired, sad, and overwhelmed. These words seem so inadequate to

---

[8] This was first published in
https://cindygreb.wordpress.com/2015/10/10/the-next-season/

convey the depth of exhaustion I was feeling. I only know that I was beyond depleted.

Fortunately, since other family members had converged to be with my mother this morning, it gave me the opportunity to indulge in some much-needed alone time. I am one of those people who needs a lot of time by myself, and I hadn't had much solitude this week.

I walked to the edge of my brother's property and down the long leaf-strewn path toward the edge of a beautiful stream. I found a large rock in a pocket of sun and sat myself down upon it.

And that's all I did.

I didn't have the energy for anything else. I didn't pray; I didn't prod myself to change or shift or buck up. I didn't try to figure anything out. I just sat.

I felt weighted and listless. My spark was completely gone.

I just sat.

Ever so slowly, the world began to work its magic on me. After maybe ten or twenty minutes, I had the energy to lift my head. I noticed more trees had changed color since the last time I'd walked to this particular spot. There was one tree with beautiful bright coral-colored leaves against a sky of radiant blue. It was breathtaking.

I began to notice leaves dancing through the air, letting go of the trees to which they had been attached for many months. They spiraled toward the creek which gently carried them downstream.

I was somewhat conscious of the beautiful metaphor of surrender unfolding all around me, but mostly I became aware that my mood was ever so slightly beginning to shift. My energy was slowly rising.

The world is a beautiful place. When I'm sad or tired, it's harder to focus on the beauty. But it's there, just waiting to uplift me whenever I take the time to immerse myself in it.

Can I help my mother release her grasp on this beautiful life so she can embrace the next even more beautiful one? I don't know. That is my prayer. My prayer is that she be at peace with the change of the seasons. Not just spring and summer, but fall and winter, too.

We cannot stop the wheel from turning. And there is no end in a wheel. There is only the next season.

A tiny and perfect arrangement of flowers growing through the cracks of a parking lot.

Unexpected Sweetness

December 4, 2015

I had had a long day at work, but before going home I found myself veering toward the nursing home where Mom was living. I thought I would "just say hi." But when I walked into her room it soon became clear this would be a very different kind of visit.

Mom was sitting slumped in her favorite chair, eyes closed. I could hear the oxygen machine making its rhythmic thrumming noise. Her dinner tray was sitting in front of her, completely untouched. When I woke her up, she was more confused than I'd ever seen her. This worried me. Mom had a lot of physical problems but she had always been really together mentally. This confusion indicated a definite "change in mental status." I was afraid it was a sign she was getting close to the end.

After a few sentences of conversation Mom somehow realized she was not making sense. Concerned, she asked me, "Am I always going to be like this?" I replied truthfully, "I don't know, Mom. I hope not."

I sat with her and talked with her and stroked her arms and her hair, little ministrations that always comforted her. When she started to seem calmer, I went to talk with the nurse to see what was going on and what, if anything, we could do.[9] Meanwhile, an aide came in to help Mom bathe and get ready for bed. Gradually she became more lucid and peaceful.

By then, it was well after 10:30 p.m. I hadn't had any dinner yet and so I asked Mom if she minded if I went home. She must have been very tired because she seemed quite okay with me leaving. (This was unusual. Usually I could never stay long enough for her.) So, having received her unexpected permission, I stood to give her one last hug for the night. I said, "I love you, Mama." (In recent years I had started to occasionally call her "mama" or "mamacita." The terms felt more affectionate than the standard "Mom.")

To my surprise and delight, I heard her reply, "I hope I get to be your mama again."

Those words touched me to my core. I couldn't have asked for a sweeter benediction.

While I happen to believe in reincarnation, my mother, I was quite sure, did not. But in that sweet state she was in, perhaps her soul came through with a truth that her conscious mind wouldn't normally be able to accept.

---

[9] We decided to get her tested for a urinary tract infection, which ended up being the culprit. This explained her uncharacteristic confusion.

Regardless, what a treasure those words were. What a blessing to hold in my heart.

Making the Choice for a Different Kind of Holiday

December 2014

Christmas Eve was just around the corner. As a teenager and adult, I preferred Christmas Eve to Christmas day. We would have a big feast (really, a copy of our Thanksgiving meal), then hurry off to the candlelight Christmas Eve service (my favorite of the year, filled with lots of singing), then come back home to host an open house. It was an evening filled to the brim with gaiety, food, family, and friends.

In more recent years, as siblings got married and had children of their own, it became increasingly rare for all of us to be together in one place at one time. Everyone was pulled in so many different directions. This would be the very first Christmas Eve we would not have dinner at Mom and Dad's house. Dad was in the nursing home now and no longer very mobile. To make matters worse, he suffered from choking unless his food was ground up. And, even if he could have eaten, Mom was no longer capable of making a huge meal (a daunting task even when one is healthy and well!) So everything was completely up in the air this Christmas. There was no consensus whatsoever of what the family would be doing. It was just catch as catch can.

The older of my two brothers would be doing things with his extended family of wife, children, grandchildren, and in-laws. My younger brother would be with his girlfriend's family. My one sister would be with her husband and daughter in their home in Georgia. Karen, meanwhile, decided to take Mom to the Christmas Eve service at Mom's favorite church.

What would I do? When I checked in with myself I realized that all I wanted to do was sit with Dad there in the nursing home. Nobody else was going to be with him, and though I didn't think he'd necessarily be conscious of the fact that it was a holiday, I found that I *wanted* to be with him. I *needed* that quiet time. I didn't want or need any of the trappings of the holiday. I didn't want to run around from one party to the next, nor did I want to be with a crowd of people. I wanted something peaceful. I wanted to sit with my dad.

And so, that's what I did. I arrived around dinner time and fed him his not terribly appetizing food. He was in a geri chair and after dinner the staff wheeled him into the hallway. It turned out that some good people were roaming the nursing home singing carols. And so I I simply sat by Dad's side, holding his hand, and singing along to the carols.

It was simple. It was peaceful. It was perfect. Nothing more was needed than the simple connection of one human being with another.

When we are caring for a beloved who is getting ready to leave this world, we need to prioritize. We need to be kind to ourselves. It is unwise to "try to do everything." It just creates too much stress. The very last thing we need is to pressure ourselves to create the "perfect holiday." That's not what Christmas (or Hanukkah or Thanksgiving or whatever) is about.

The Spirit of Christmas is love. Be with the people you love. Nothing else really matters.

Sometimes It All Becomes Too Much

2008

I'd been working as a hospice chaplain in Santa Fe, New Mexico for two years. I usually had a caseload of forty clients at any given time. But then our hospice merged with another much larger corporate entity. In an effort to cut costs, several staff members were laid off or fired. Unfortunately, the bereavement counselor was one of them. I was asked to assume her duties as well as my own. Suddenly my caseload and workload doubled.

Like most of my colleagues who were also picking up the slack of a greatly reduced staff, I was exhausted. Besides the larger number of clients and the greater amount of paperwork and responsibilities, for a while I was also commuting over an hour and a half each way to cover for a chaplain in Albuquerque who was on vacation for several weeks. And on top of all that, one especially lovely client was nearing death.

But then an opportunity presented itself. A national conference for hospice social workers, spiritual counselors, and bereavement counselors was to be held in Albuquerque. It was so close by, how could I not go? As a bonus, a very dear friend from Philadelphia, also a hospice chaplain, would be attending.

As with most conferences, there were both keynote speakers to listen to as well as smaller workshops to attend. But one thing I didn't expect to find was a labyrinth--inside the conference center!

I entered the room where a large labyrinth, painted on canvas, had been unrolled on the floor. Whoever had arranged for this age-old sacred ritual to be part of the conference had done a superb job of creating sacred space. The lighting was dim, there were lovely plants everywhere, there were opportunities for placing prayer request "leaves" on a great tree hanging on the wall, and the room was a blessed no-talking zone. I could feel my body gratefully settling into the silence.

Finally I felt ready. I stepped up to the entrance of the labyrinth. I waited for a few moments and then slowly began to take steps on the circuitous path.

I had been walking less than five minutes when my sobs started. It was so unexpected. There I was, in the middle of this quiet room, crying. I couldn't seem to stop.

I was surprised because I had had umpteen clients die over the course of my employment in this particular hospice thus far, and I hadn't yet shed any tears. This was actually a bit bewildering because I was known among my friends as an emotional person. In my home church in Pennsylvania, I was one of the members occasionally asked to speak for ten minutes or so on any given Sunday. When I was up there at the podium sharing my heart, I would often find myself quite verklempt, and sobs would start to erupt. Friends in the congregation would smile, knowing this emotional release was not unusual for me. And I, embarrassed, would laugh through my tears. But somehow in this hospice job I'd been able to maintain a professional veneer. My emotions had been held in check.

But no longer! It was as if all the cumulative losses had suddenly become too much. The dam had broken. It was time for the tears to flow.

This is not an unusual phenomenon for grieving people--even ones like me who were unaware of the fact. Many people can face grief stoically for quite a while. Then something happens and they are cracked open.

We need to give ourselves and each other permission to be wherever we are in this journey of grief. I think society often expects people to be very sad for a while and then to "get over it." But sometimes the pattern is reversed. Sometimes people will appear "okay" for quite a while and then, months later, the grief will really hit. Another scenario is that the sadness and pain will ebb and flow, interspersed with seeming normalcy.

The only thing predictable about grief is its unpredictability. Every person is different; every relationship is unique; and so the process of grieving will also be different for each person.

Just allow. Allow the tears when they're ready. And don't judge if they're not there. It's all okay. It's all okay.

The Message of Silent Tears[10]

March 28, 2019

I have been living in New Mexico and recently suffering the effects of an excess of juniper pollen. Either my eyes itch until I frantically rub them raw, or finally my over-the-counter meds kick in enough to tone down the itching to a dull ache. When this happens, instead of itching, often my eyes will just leak tears.

I assume this is a good thing. My body is trying to rid itself of this alien invader, this totally natural substance that feels completely foreign to this eastern-born-and-bred woman.

As I note these silent tears, I am reminded of other times when silent tears ran down my cheeks. The first instance I remember happened on May 5, 1995. You may be wondering why I remember the exact date. It's because it was my first wedding anniversary post-marital break-up.

Interestingly, my mind had not been aware of the date that day. But when I went to church that Sunday morning, shortly into the service I noticed tears were streaming down my face. I was not

---

[10] The bulk of this was written as a blog post here:
https://www.cynthiagreb.com/the-message-of-silent-tears/

crying audibly, and there was not anything obviously emotional or moving going on around me. I was quite puzzled, especially as the tears continued to flow for perhaps twenty minutes or so. I finally whispered to the friend sitting next to me, "I don't know why these tears keep falling down my face." That's when she told me it was my anniversary. How did she know, you may wonder? She was my ex-husband's girlfriend. He must have mentioned it to her that morning.

I hasten to add, lest you think badly of my ex,[11] that they got together a couple of months *after* he and I faced the sad fact that our marriage seemed to be broken. To be honest, I don't know that he and I were necessarily irrevocably broken, but we had been suffering for many long months. And even though we still loved one another, I finally received a message that we were meant to let go.

I find it extremely interesting that my mind didn't remember the date, but my soul clearly did.

This silent tear phenomenon happened a second time when I received a message from my father after he died. (See the chapter "An Angel Gets His Wings" beginning on page 134.) And then it happened a third time in September of last year.

---

[11] I hate that term, "ex." It erases all our years together and feels so... permanent and angry. I am not angry at him and I don't think he's angry at me. We are no longer married, but that doesn't cancel out all the many years of love.

I had been in the second week of a pilgrimage, this soul-driven journey that my intuition had prodded me to embark upon. I had been driving on this very curvy, very narrow mountain road for perhaps 45 minutes. I had encountered only about two cars. I was on a long section of the road which boasted no homes, no crossroads, and no driveways. Trees, grasses, and a few wildflowers... that was all I saw. Until, seemingly out of nowhere, I noticed this rather ornate gate and several beautifully built stone buildings which reminded me of a national monument or perhaps a museum or visitors center. It was none of the above. Instead I saw a sign which read "Yurok Veterans Cemetery."

As my pilgrimage was a sacred journey, I felt compelled to stop and offer prayers. The gate was locked but there were some small boulders on the right side of the short driveway. I parked my car off to the side, dug around in a box on the passenger seat for my rattle, and got out and sat on one of those rocks.

After a few moments, I began to shake my rattle and pray. As is typical for me when I am outside, I sang my prayers. I sang out a welcome to the spirits of the land. I probably greeted the air, the sun, the trees, the flowers, and the waters. And then I sang to the spirits of those who were buried there. I thanked them for their service and I prayed that they had been appreciated. I prayed, too, for those who loved them. I don't remember exactly all that I prayed, but what I surely do remember is that within moments of beginning my prayers, silent tears started rolling down my cheeks. And those tears streamed for the entire length of my prayers.

What did those tears mean? Clearly my soul was remembering or feeling something. I wonder if perhaps I had been a part of this particular tribe in a former lifetime. I don't think I'd ever heard much about the Yurok people prior to this visit, even though I later learned they are the largest tribe in California. But I'm guessing there is some deep soul connection between me and them.

I am grateful for tears. Eyes are said to be a window into the soul. If so, perhaps then tears are a way for our souls to communicate with us. Perhaps, like my allergy-related tears, they provide a cleansing and a healing.

If you find these silent tears happening to you, just let them flow. Your soul obviously needs to release some important emotions.

Part II

WHEN LOVED ONES

ARE DYING

Goodbye House, Goodbye Dad[12]

February 2014

I had been staying in the home of friends while I was back in Pennsylvania visiting and caring for my parents, but eventually it became clear I needed to give my friends their space. I decided to temporarily move into the room I had lived in as a teenager. It was the family home, although my family no longer lived there. The kids were all grown and my parents had both recently moved into a nursing home—my father because of the progression of Alzheimer's disease, and my mother because there was no longer enough money for the caregivers we'd hired to assist her plus all the other expenses of maintaining this rather large home.

In addition to spending time with both my parents, I needed to help sell, sort through, and dispose of all the remaining family possessions so that the bank could take possession of the family home. It wasn't a case of foreclosure; it was because we'd had to get a reverse mortgage to pay for my parents' care. And with them no longer at home, the house had to go to the bank. To say

---

[12] First published under the title "The House that Cried" in
https://cindygreb.wordpress.com/2014/04/02/the-house-that-cried/
Reprinted, with permission, in:
http://www.incareofdad.com/blog/goodbye-house-goodbye-dad/

this was a time of great change for the Greb family would be an understatement.

I walked in the front door loaded down with my luggage. And I stood there, gazing around in total shock. My siblings had told me about the pipe that had burst about two weeks before, but there was no way I could've prepared myself for what lay in shambles around me. Apparently the thermostat had been set at about 50 degrees, but one particular bedroom hung over an open porch and I guess the radiator pipes couldn't hold up to the record cold temperatures.

Large sections of hardwood floor had been pulled up. Drywall had been torn down. Rusty looking stains ran down the hall walls. Wainscoting had been removed. Insulation had been ripped out. One closet had been completely ruined. Furniture and other items had been moved from the damaged areas and stuffed into adjacent rooms. There was a layer of dust everywhere from the work my brother and the clean-up crew had begun. Several large fans were on at full blast and the living room still reeked of mold and mildew. It was a big house and it looked like a good third of it had been ruined. And the rest of it was looking none too good either.

Stunned, I went about putting my things away. Then I attended to my next order of business: finding one room of the house that was still clean enough to support an altar for my daily meditations. I settled on the piano room. I set up a card table and covered it with a beautiful scarf. I placed some sacred items upon the cloth, found a candle, pulled up a chair, and lit the candle.

As I sat before the flame and took a few breaths, I became aware of how sad I was. I felt stunned by the devastation and destruction around me. I decided to talk out loud to the house. What the heck; I was all alone. Why not?

Within a few minutes my one-sided conversation had turned into a song. I was singing to the house when a thought popped into my head. Our house was sad. It had burst into tears because everyone was suddenly gone and it lay empty. Its tears had flooded the house.

My song turned into a lament. I keened and keened, filled with sorrow for this poor house. This dear house had been lovingly built by my father's own hands when his burgeoning family had outgrown the small one-story house we'd grown up in. This house had once been filled with my parents, my three siblings, and then a fourth sibling—my youngest brother, newly born to my mother when we had just moved into the house.

It had been the family home for forty years. It had seen thousands of meals served, scores of holidays celebrated, and parties and picnics hosted. It had heard the laughter and conversation of friends, relatives, and visitors. There had been the pitter-patter of a dog, several cats, six grandchildren, and one great grandchild. Later, after the last of the children and one foster child had moved out, it had held a rotating roster of boarders, grandchildren who needed a place to stay, adult children who were having temporary marital or financial problems, and eventually, caregivers who became an integral and loving part of the family. So much life! So much love! So much laughter! And suddenly, all of it was gone.

When first Dad, and then Mom moved into the nursing home, the house was suddenly empty. There was no more husband and wife in the home, no more visiting children or grandchildren, no more friends, no more caregivers, no more love and laughter. And no one had said goodbye to this dear house. No one had said thank you. The house no longer had a purpose to serve. It was still holding possessions, but all the life was gone from it.

I wailed. No one was home so I could be as loud as I needed to be. I cried and cried and cried. I cried for the house that no longer felt like a home. I cried for all the changes. I cried that we would no longer have a family home to gather in. I cried for my mother who was no longer in the home in which she had raised her five children and found her purpose for living. And I cried especially for my father because I knew he was dying.

My poor father. He had begged us to keep this home in the family. He wanted it to be available for the grandchildren or for anyone in the family who would ever need a place to stay. And now not only could we not honor his request, but he himself was no longer here in this home. He was in a bed, in a nursing home, asleep more than awake, barely eating, getting more and more gaunt, speaking less and less, and suffering all the indignities of elders who have to depend on others to take care of their most basic needs. My poor, dear, wonderful father.

Dad died thirty hours later.

I hadn't expected him to die then. I knew he was headed in that direction, but none of us expected him to die that weekend.

Maybe my unexpected outpouring of grief helped to release him. Just like the house's "tears" helped to release my own.

I have had so many blessings in my life it would be impossible to count them all. Living in that home with a family that loved one another was certainly a very big one. Being raised by good parents was a huge one. Having a father who worked so hard but so willingly, who loved so unabashedly, who laughed and played and prayed with equal abandon, is absolutely a blessing beyond compare.

Goodbye, House. Goodbye, Dad. I love you.

The Last Three Months[13]

April 20, 2015

There are so many wonderful things to remember about Dad, but sadly, I seem to be stuck in an endless review of his last few months.

If he had started to drastically decline and then simply continued that decline, I think I could have accepted that. After all, death comes to each one of us, and after several years suffering the indignities of Alzheimer's, I'm sure at some level he was more than ready to let go of this life. But Dad's health and mental clarity kept cycling up and down, up and down. I could never be sure whether he was near death or simply going through another dip in his cycle.

When Dad was admitted to the nursing home in November of 2013, he had definitely declined further, but he was still walking, talking, and eating. Then he fell and hit his head and suddenly he couldn't walk or eat on his own any more. He also began to exhibit very bad tremoring, shaking and the sudden jerking

---

[13] First published as "Deathiversaries and Post-Death Birthdays" in https://cindygreb.wordpress.com/2015/04/20/deathiversaries-and-post-death-birthdays/

which his doctor believed was an indication of advanced Parkinson's.

The jerking was heartbreaking to see because it had come on so suddenly and it completely interrupted his ability to rest. Rest had always been very important to Dad, but even more so as his Alzheimer's escalated. It was as if he just needed to escape from the world for a while because it had become way too confusing for him. For a while, he was sleeping, off and on, about fifteen hours a day.

Because of those horrible jerks, we started Dad on a medication that relaxed his body so the involuntary movements would cease. But unfortunately it also meant he was mentally rather "out of it" a large portion of the day. The nurses hated giving him that medication because just as he was coming back to himself, talking and joking around, it was time for the next dose. We didn't know what to do. But it seemed he was safer and calmer, as well as more rested, so we opted to keep him on it.

Then something happened that took the matter out of our hands. He fell into a bad fever. He became so weak he could no longer safely eat anything. Even drinking became hazardous. And so they had to discontinue the med. It just wasn't safe to administer it.

And then, miracle of miracles, after a week or so, he got better! His eyes were open and he was talking again! We were so relieved. And the symptoms which the doctor had attributed to Parkinson's never came back!

By this time, we had put Dad on hospice care. Because of the lingering effects from the fall, his prolonged fever, and his lack of food, the weakness had become pronounced. Once in a while the staff tried to walk him down the hall, an aide on each side and one behind him with the wheelchair in case he needed it. But generally he was in bed or in a geri-chair.

Then Dad began to get a bedsore. This often happens when people are sitting or lying down most of the time and not getting sufficient nutrients or circulation. Dad had always had a great appetite--for both food and life--but, let's face it, most nursing homes do not provide great food. We would have brought him many of his meals from home or restaurants except for the fact that he had become at risk for choking. Because of this all his food needed to be ground up. Of course he lost his appetite! How appealing is ground up meat or pureed peas or corn or carrots? He could no longer have bread or any deserts except ice cream or applesauce. No wonder this hale and hearty 5'-11" man had become so gaunt.

During all this time I continued to agonize. *Should we take him off hospice so he could get some physical therapy?* (Medicare, Medicaid, and other insurance companies generally don't approve physical therapy if someone is actively dying.) *Did he have a chance at recovering if we pushed him a bit? Would he be able to walk again? Should we try to take him out to breakfast?* Going out for breakfast was one of his favorite things in the world. It could potentially greatly lift his spirits.

Dad kept going up and down, up and down. I could never figure out exactly if he was dying or just going through a bad spell. I kept on second-guessing our choices. Finally I called the hospice social worker and left a message asking about whether or not we should take him off hospice so we could get him into physical therapy again.

Then he came down with another fever.

It would be his last one.

I had assumed this fever would be similar to the last one–unpleasant, but temporary. Instead it was one of several signs of his approaching death. I wish the hospice staff or one of the nurses had recognized the signs and given us a heads-up so we could have been around him while he was still conscious that last day. I wish *I* had recognized the signs. At some level, I knew that fever was one of the physical signs that death was imminent. [14] But I was either in denial or too tired to think straight.

---

[14] There are many sources which delineate symptoms to look for as someone nears death. This is a particularly good one:
http://www.abchospice.com/Websites/abchospice/Images/ABC%20Resources/preparing%20for%20death.pdf

I had been with Dad for about six hours the day before he died. After I noticed his fever, the nurses gave him something to make him more comfortable. Eventually he appeared to be resting and less agitated. Because I was tired and naturally assuming I'd see him the next morning, I left.

I wish I had stayed.

I'm sure a lot of us do this when our loved ones pass. We wonder what we could have done differently. We wish we had been there more, voiced our love, withheld our anger. Fortunately, I know Dad knew how much I loved him. And I'm grateful we only had one fight with one another in my whole life. That's not bad. I realize that's a tremendous gift. But I still wish I had been with him throughout those last 24 hours.

I have been having trouble letting go of those last three months of his life. I haven't been able to let myself be at peace about it all.

Perhaps writing this right now will help to shift that.

P.S. Here is the Grace part. A couple days after writing this, I was amazed to notice that I *did* feel better. Somehow my sad obsession with wishing I could have done things differently, lifted. It seemed to help me to acknowledge it all instead of keeping it locked inside like some big dark secret.

Blessed grace. What a relief.

The Labor of Death

Unless there's a sudden trauma,

dying is labor. It's clearly labor.

The breathing becomes more rapid,

almost a panting.

However, instead of laboring to enter this world

from the comfortable confines of the womb,

there is the labor to exit this world.

There is a struggle as the self gradually allows the soul

to separate from the familiar home of the body.

Except the body is not a home;

it is more like a cage

or a very heavy coat

encasing a soul whose nature it is to fly.

But we forget that.

We cling to the body because it's all we know.

It's all we've known our whole life long.

We forget.

We forget what it was like before we slipped into the womb

to begin this life.

If only we could remember.

If only we could remember

how very different dying would be.[15]

---

[15] First published:
https://cindygreb.wordpress.com/2016/02/08/labor-of-death/

Helen and the Lion (Breaking Free)

February 2016

Helen was Lisa's mother. Lisa was a friend who had called to ask if I would be willing to be one of two people to care for Helen in the nighttime hours. I agreed.

I liked Helen. I met her near the end of her life when maybe she wasn't quite as sharp as she had once been, but she was still a delightful person. Often she was willing to sit right next to me, even though she didn't know me. Sometimes sitting there, she'd hold my hand, which I found very sweet. She was also quite independent considering she had no car, an unsteady gait, and a mind that was not quite as functional as it used to be. Her whole life at the time existed basically within the confines of a small apartment in an assisted living facility.

Over the course of just a little over a month, this paper thin woman with no appetite began to slip ever closer to the final days of her life. I had been invited to sleep on the couch or on an air mattress during my hours there, but I found that impossible. I had to keep ever alert because at any moment Helen was likely to quietly get up from her bed--even with rails up and an alarmed mat on the floor--and walk precariously toward the bathroom just around the corner of her bedroom door. Apparently she had fallen more than once in recent months, and I didn't want her to fall on my watch.

At about night #40 of my caregiving duties, Helen was breathing rapidly, just like those who are getting close to death often do. I sat next to her bed and held her hand. Eventually I realized she seemed a bit agitated. It appeared that me holding her hand was not what she wanted at that time. So I got up and walked into the living room where I laid down on the sofa. I was just a few feet away from her on the other side of her bedroom wall. I'd be able to hear if anything happened.

After many, many nights of interrupted sleep, my body briefly succumbed to slumber and, quite unexpectedly, to a most magnificent dream.

> Lisa and I are keeping watch over Helen. I see a large majestic lion launching himself from Helen's bedroom, through her window, great wings unfurled. As he passes over the threshold he changes from a creature of black and white into a glorious technicolored being.

What a beautiful message. This world cannot hold back the spirit of one such as Helen! No, she will not be stopped. When her spirit is ready, she will fly! As she leaves this world of three-dimensional superficiality, she will emerge into a glorious new world of beauty and color and splendor. Nothing can hold back the great lionhearted Helen!

A few scants months prior to my job caring for Helen, I had been honored to officiate at my dear niece's memorial service. I spoke of the threshold between this world and the next. I spoke of how our bodies stand at that threshold, usually broken and frail, and then, when the spirit is ready, we step over the threshold and, arms aloft, prepare to fly into the heavens.

But now I realize this metaphor of the flying lion is infinitely more powerful. Because when a lion leaps, there is so much strength and power in those hind legs. When a lion leaps, there is great intention and focus and absolutely no hesitation. Lions don't leap for the heck of it, they leap because they want to get somewhere very specific.

Helen's spirit was ready. She both leapt *and* flew! Gravity had no more hold on her. She was more than ready for the next world.

May we all be so ready.

Emotional Triage (The Story of Andy)

February 2009

When caring for loved ones, often we have to make extremely difficult choices. My heart is especially thinking of those women (let's face it, it's usually the women) who are caring for both parents and children. How does one make the choice between those who gave you life and those you brought into the world?

In my case, I didn't have any children to worry about except an adult stepson who was doing well. But I had two parents on the east coast and a number of caregiving clients in the Southwest. My parents had to take priority, clearly, but that didn't mean it wasn't very difficult to surrender the care of beloved clients into others' hands.

When my mother had her heart attack in early 2009, followed two days later by a small stroke, it became immediately apparent that I needed to move back to Pennsylvania in order to help with Mom's care and rehabilitation. Unfortunately, this meant I'd have to make a very challenging call to my favorite hospice client and friend who lived in New Mexico, 2000 miles away.

Andy was a woman--a real firecracker, a former trucker and the first female bartender in her town. On the day that I was introduced to Andy, there was an immediate connection. There she stood, dressed casually in slacks and a top, tethered to her oxygen machine as I approached. We both grinned. We were quite different in many ways, but there was no doubt we'd become fast friends.

Hospice chaplains are required to make a minimal number of visits to those clients open to it. Most clients received pastoral visits once or twice a week. But I often visited Andy three times a week. Why? She didn't have much emotional support. She was a widow who had two adult sons. One was a good guy but he suffered from a pretty serious drug addiction. Andy loved him dearly, but he wasn't capable of caring for his mom; instead she was often bailing him out in one way or another. Her other son was a really good son, but he lived four hours away and often had issues of his own to contend with. Andy had only one remaining friend in the area, a neighbor who was a little "slow." Other than that, she was on her own.

I became a bit of a lifeline for her. She was extremely grateful to have someone to talk with. Unfortunately, in spite of our comradery and close emotional bonds, I consider her my biggest failure as a chaplain. Andy believed in God, but she was scared of death. In fact, I find myself wanting to say 'She was scared to death of death.' No matter what I said, how I counseled, what scriptures or books I read to her or referred to, I couldn't help her to trust that there was great love and beauty on the other side of this earthly veil. I couldn't seem to transfer to her my absolute faith in an afterlife. She was completely stuck in her fear.

As her physical condition started to worsen, there were more and more times when she had trouble breathing. Her nurse would advise her to take a little bit of morphine, which is valuable not only for pain but for assisting with shortness of breath. But Andy was afraid of morphine. She was terrified it would accelerate her dying process. No amount of education on the part of the nurse could assuage her fears.

Andy's fears, of course, made her symptoms even worse. Have you ever noticed that when you're afraid, your breathing becomes extremely shallow? Andy was in a vicious cycle. She was ill and her unabated fears made all her symptoms worse. Instead of morphine, the default drug for Andy became Ativan, a medication which helped to ease her anxiety when it got out of control.

Andy was eventually admitted to a nursing home because it was thought it might be better for her if she were closer to those who could administer meds when she needed them. (The hospice office was 45 minutes away, and because New Mexico is so rural and the territory over which we traveled was vast, it would often be a couple of hours or more before a nurse could get to her.) Unfortunately, the nurses at the particular nursing facility where she'd been moved to were overworked and not as attentive to Andy's comfort level as they could have been.

Andy was in the nursing home when I had to call her and give her the bad news that my mother had had a heart attack and that I felt I needed to stay with her. What a terribly difficult call that was. I had been unable to help Andy get beyond her fears, and now when she needed support more than ever, I wouldn't be there. I'm sure it appeared to her that I was "abandoning" her.

I pleaded with her to understand. This was my mother. *How could I not be with my mother?* Dear Andy had no choice but to accept my choice.

She died while I was in Pennsylvania helping with the care of my parents.

It was heartbreaking.

This is one of those stories that I can't wrap up with a happy ending. Andy died alone, in pain, and afraid. The only thing I could do was pray, from very far away. (Though of course distance is irrelevant when it comes to prayer.)

We want things to be easy and happy for those we love. And, sometimes we are completely powerless to provide the comfort and ease we yearn to give. This is where faith comes in. Though the end of Andy's life was not easy, I have to remember that much of her life was very good. She had had a wonderful husband and two well-loved sons. Her life had been interesting. I have to remind myself that when she moved on to the celestial realms, more comfort would be available to her.

I believe there is great grace as souls transition. I have come to believe that some souls, after leaving their physical bodies, require a lot of time to heal from the trauma they endured during their last hours, days, months, or years on Earth. And they are mercifully given that time to rest and recover. Eventually, these souls become open to receiving all the love, all the joy, and all the peace that heaven offers. Our prayers can absolutely help them in this process.

Bless you, Andy. I am grateful for your enduring friendship. And I pray that, finally, at long last, you are at peace.

Letting Go (The Story of Mary)

February 2014

Mary was a client, a beautiful woman around 68 years old. When she was younger, she looked like a movie star. Her husband was unspeakably proud of her beauty, but also of her spiritual gifts. They were soulmates who came together later in Vince's life, after his first marriage had ended and at a time when he never expected to find love again.

When I met Mary, her pretty blonde hair had turned white, but her eyes were still a gorgeous blue. Sometimes, after I'd helped her to bathe, she'd sit on her four-legged walker looking in the bathroom mirror as I stood behind her combing and blow drying her hair. I would look at her reflection and think, *She looks like a mermaid.* A beautiful, elder white-haired mermaid.

I have never before or since had those thoughts about anyone.

Mary's husband, Vince, was a retired physician. He had been given my name by a colleague, a friend who referred caregivers to those families in the area who needed one. On the day of my interview, as soon as I walked in the door, I felt a sense of comfort with both of them. Vince and I immediately became friends. The relationship with Mary took a bit longer to build only because her natural introversion was compounded by an inability to communicate well--either verbally or with facial expressions. This was one of several sad afflictions that were the result of a rather uncommon disease called progressive supranuclear palsy.

As Mary's condition worsened, her mobility and strength were greatly compromised. When I met them, Vince had been her sole caregiver for several years. As time wore on, the physical and emotional stress of caring for her full-time became challenging, especially due to his own heart condition. (I have so much respect for those who valiantly help their loved one day in and day out even when they have troubles of their own.) Eventually he realized he would need to have some assistance, if only for a few hours a week. It was decided that I would come three times a week in order to do some household chores as well as help Mary take a shower, get dressed, and lay down for an afternoon nap. Meanwhile, Vince would run into town to do some errands and simply to get out of the house and out among people.

Mary and I became good friends. She and Vince had once lived in a spiritual community in Oklahoma, but here in this tiny Colorado mountain town, with her limited abilities, her social circle had sadly dwindled to include only her husband. She began to enjoy our times together as our conversations gradually became more and more like that of two girlfriends.

Twice during the course of my employment with them, Vince had to drive four hours away for a medical appointment. He would be gone from early morning until night and so I was to be Mary's companion and helper on those days. My favorite memory of those times was sitting with her watching romantic comedies on Netflix, a pleasure she had never had before as Vince's tastes ran more toward documentaries and the history channel. Mary was a deeply romantic soul, and the woman in her thrilled to the stories of blossoming love. (Her favorite was "Ever After," a modern telling of the Cinderella story, starring Drew Barrymore.)

Vince was an exceptional caregiver of his beloved wife. He helped her with every aspect of her care--making sure she took her meds; preparing all her (exceedingly healthy) meals--including making homemade bread in the bread machine twice a week as well as regularly baking gluten-free chocolate cookies; helping her dress; helping her to the toilet several times a day; doing her laundry; and faithfully guiding her through a thorough ten-minute oral care regime a couple times a day. He was so devoted.

After several years of their daily routine, one morning Mary had a mental break. It was the straw that broke the camel's back for Vince. Suddenly he just couldn't do it anymore. All of a sudden all the neverending hours of care had become too much.

In desperation, Vince called a friend of his, a physician who specialized in geriatric care. This good man arranged for Mary to be admitted to a hospital one hour's drive away.

To be honest, I was amazed Vince lasted as long as he did. Until you have experienced caring for a loved one day in and day out, morning, noon, and night, you cannot imagine the depth of fatigue that can build up over time. I know of other good people, including myself, who came to this same exact breaking point.[16]

That morning Vince called me to see if I could come over and help. I had never heard him sound so stressed. Of course I rushed over. I was able to get Mary up and dressed for the hour-long drive to the hospital. I drove while the long-married couple sat in the back, grabbing some final time together before the long separation that was about to occur.

I stayed with them both during the surprisingly long admission process, which took the better part of the day. Then later that night, in extremely dark and foggy conditions, I drove Vince

---

[16] Mine happened in the year 2010, after sixteen months of living with and caring for both parents. I was so glad to be there for them, but after several months of both day and night duty, I was exhausted to the core and depressed. When Mom insisted on shopping one day and then almost collapsed in the store, with nowhere available to sit down, I reached my limit.
I was so unbearably stressed. Later that day I broke down sobbing in my sister-in-law's arms. I kept saying, "I can't do it anymore. I can't do it anymore." And that's when we finally decided to dip into my parents' savings and hire some caregivers.

home, where he would lie in bed alone, without his beloved Mary, for the first time ever in their married life.

This was such a cataclysmic change for them. Everything in me wanted to be with Mary to help her adjust to her new surroundings. Unfortunately, I had a flight to catch. I was headed back home to be with my parents. Dad wasn't doing very well.

I called both Vince and Mary a few times from Pennsylvania. Mary was usually asleep when I called. Vince reported that she was spending lots of time in silent meditation, as she had done during her naps when she was home. Mary had a beautiful ability to enter an almost a trancelike state of consciousness during which she would commune with her beloved Yeshua.[17] Her relationships with both Vince and Yeshua sustained her in a life which, from the outside, appeared increasingly small. Eventually I realized that perhaps this time in the nursing home, away from Vince and her regular routine, might actually have been a blessing in disguise because it enabled her to spend hours upon hours in blissful communion with Christ. What better way to prepare for the next world!

While Mary was in the nursing home, Vince was recovering from his intense exhaustion. His own health had greatly deteriorated

---

[17] "Yeshua" is the Hebrew name for the man most of us know as Jesus. Here is one site that explains it:
https://allthatsinteresting.com/yeshua-jesus-real-name

during the previous few months of caring for Mary. He wisely gave himself the time and space to rest.

I had wanted so much to support both of these dear people during this poignant time of transition in their lives, but once again I needed to prioritize my own family. I had little choice but to love Mary and Vince from afar.

It's tough to love multiple people scattered in different parts of the world when we only have the ability to be in one place at a time. This is when prayer comes in handy. It also helps to have the humility to acknowledge that people can function without us! (I confess this has been problematic for me. While I don't necessarily think myself indispensable, I do often feel like I am greatly needed.)

While I was there in Pennsylvania with my folks, I got word that a client had passed. Vera had become very dear to me and I was very, very disappointed that I wouldn't be back in time for her memorial service. Then another friend--a woman close to my age whom I didn't even realize was that sick--died as well. And then, sadly, I got a third call--the call I had hoped not to get. Dear Mary had also passed through the veil. I was so sad.

Three friends from my Colorado home had died within a short span of one or two weeks. As with Andy, I hadn't been able to be with them at the end. Unfortunately, that was just the way it was. I had no choice but to surrender. I couldn't change what had happened and it did no good to hold onto guilt.

Fortunately, my return flight at least got me back in time for Mary's service.

When it comes to death, we can never know the day nor the hour. It is a decision made by God and the soul of the departed. Those of us who remain have no choice but to accept this divine timing. We may or may not be ready. It doesn't matter.

After both my nineteen-year-old niece and my mother died in late 2015, for the first time ever, I decided to consult a medium. (I discovered, quite by accident, that my psychic friend, Jean, was also a gifted medium. I had had no idea!)[18] One of the things my niece said during that session with Jean was that there was no need for regret or anger about the cause of her death because "it was just my time."

We each have "our time."

Loving someone who is nearing the end means letting go over and over again. It is out of our hands. We can rail against it, or we can allow ourselves to come to a cautious peace about it. Their soul needed to leave because "it was time." Our job is to

---

[18] Jean Westbrook, https://www.circleofwaterlight.com/ (She lives in Doylestown, PA but can and does also do readings by phone.)

celebrate and honor the life that they lived, to continue to love them, and to learn to carry on, grief and all.

Making Peace with Her Dying[19]
(The Story of Vera)

January 30, 2014

Today I received word that a friend was nearing the end. She had begun walking that brave lonely road.

Vera had had several false starts on this road before, but this time her daughter-in-law told me it felt different. She was now refusing food and drink. So yes, it seems my friend has chosen her time and it is fast approaching.

When I heard the news I felt heartsick, not necessarily because she would be leaving this earthly plane, for I understand our time here is limited. I was sad because I was 2000 miles away and the earliest I could possibly get to her would be, at minimum, eight days away. I was sad because, in five short months, she and I had become dear friends and because there was love between us and because I wanted to be there to offer comfort if I could and because I wanted to say goodbye.

---

[19] First published as
https://cindygreb.wordpress.com/2015/01/30/making-peace-with-her-dying/

Vera is one of two women I helped care for over the course of this past year. Most of the time she didn't need a lot of support---some assistance bathing, some simple meal preparation, some support walking, or when she was especially weak, transferring to and from a wheelchair. In between these tasks and some simple cleaning, we would chat. We enjoyed one another. It didn't matter that we were 35 years apart in age.

One of Vera's favorite things was when I massaged her feet. She had never experienced that particular luxury before I came into her life. Without fail, it would make her purr with delight. I also massaged her hands and eventually even her head. She was surprised how delicious a good head rub could be. Of course I had to be especially careful not to ruin her lovely white-curled coiffure.

My favorite memory of Vera is the time I drove her to a diner forty minutes away. She and I are residents in a little town of approximately 1000 people. There are three restaurants in town, only one of which I knew was to her particular liking. So I decided it would be a grand adventure for us to travel to this particular diner instead.

This particular eating establishment was run by a woman, probably in her early 60's, who knew how to make some good, decent food, and even better, bake some incredibly delicious breads and pies.[20] So, that day Vera and I had the pleasure of

---

[20] 4th Street Diner and Bakery, Saguache, Colorado
https://www.yelp.com/biz/4th-street-diner-and-bakery-saguache-2

chatting amiably while driving through the great San Luis Valley of Colorado and then continuing to enjoy one another's company while sampling some truly tasty soup, toast, French fries, and delicious homemade pie. Great comfort food. She loved it; I loved it.

When I heard the news about Vera's recent downturn this afternoon, I sat for a while in the car in the driveway and allowed the sadness to fill me up. I wanted to honor the feelings. I didn't want to rush from this sad news right into some other activity. Then, while sitting there, I noticed the branches of the trees against a blue sky and the colorful collection of birds and squirrels munching on birdseed. I then made a conscious decision to allow myself to feel a spark of gladness. There can be both sadness and gladness all in the course of a few breaths. Sometimes it's a choice we make.

When I was ready to come inside, I was greeted by the cacophonous joy of the two dogs in my care who wildly adore me. It's hard to be sad amidst all that lovestruck jumping and wagging. I let the dogs outside and then I sat in a chair in a welcome patch of sun shining through the front door. I practiced breathing in and out, like a gentle wave rolling up on the beach and then pausing for a moment before sliding back into the sea. I sat in that lovely sun, which had been hiding for many wintry days, and I knew that whether I was able to be there or not, all would be well. It was clearly out of my hands. Vera would leave when she and God decided the time was right. And Vera would know I loved her whether I was physically present or not.

As ancient mystic Julian of Norwich once said, "All shall be well, and all shall be well, and all manner of thing shall be well."

Part III

GRACE AFTER DEATH

Today We Bury Dad

February 20, 2019

This morning I think

'Today we're burying Dad.'

I burst into tears.

I walk outside.

The sun is shining.

Birds are singing.

Maybe I'll plant flowers

On his grave.

He'd like that.

A Farewell Ritual

Written November 2018
Took place December 9, 2015

Sometimes people take a long time to leave their body. They may linger in a coma or in a state of general debilitation for days, weeks, or even months before their souls are ready to lift off into the next world. In fact, some people say the soul has already started to explore other planes and is barely present with the body at all during the last days.

My mother chose a different path.

My brother Brian and I had both been visiting with Mom one evening in the nursing home. We sat with her as she ate dinner and then we watched television together. She was quite chipper and content that day and, as always, very happy to be with any of her children.

After *Jeopardy*, Brian took his leave to go eat dinner, having come over directly after a hard day of work as a builder. After he left, Mom told me she wanted to go for a ride around the halls in her wheelchair.

First we went two doors down to look in on her friend Josephine, a fun and feisty blind woman in her 90's who hung out with Mom on a daily basis. But she appeared to already be in bed, so we moved on. We made the rounds through the two halls that made up Mom's floor and, not really seeing anyone to talk to, we returned to her room. Mom needed to go to the bathroom and I assisted her as I had hundreds of times before.

When she was finished, she stood and, as always, I helped her pull up her pants. Uncharacteristically, I was off to her side and not in front of her as is the proper protocol. I heard her softly utter the words, "Oh no." She was starting to lose her balance and I scrambled past the wheelchair to catch her as her body took a half turn and twirled to the floor like a leaf.

I was able to cushion her fall. It was very gentle, like a slide, not a great kerplunk. She hadn't hit her head, and yet when I called her name, her eyes had this scary vacant look. A part of me realized she was probably gone, but my heart wasn't ready to accept it.

I rushed out of the room to look for the nurse and, as it so happened, she was almost right outside the door, dispensing evening meds. I said breathlessly, "Mom fell." The nurse rushed in, angry with me that I hadn't waited for staff to come take her to the bathroom. (With only two staff on during the evening shift and many patients to prepare for bed, she and I both well knew Mom and I could've been waiting for half an hour for someone to answer the call bell. And Mom no longer had the ability to hold her urine that long.)

The nurse got down on the floor next to Mom and started calling her name, "Barbara! Barbara!" She continued to call, louder and louder, but of course there was no response. The nurse asked me to please leave the bathroom and give her some room.

I walked down the hallway. I didn't know what to do. My heart was pounding with the knowledge that Mom had probably already left her body. I just paced as I waited for the nurse to finish her ministrations. After about fifteen minutes, one of the aides came to tell me I could come see Mom. Then she told me what I already knew. Mom was gone.

My first order of business, I knew, was to call Brian to give him the sad and totally unexpected news. I would call the others, too, of course, but I knew it would be hardest for him, and not only because he had just left the nursing home a scant thirty minutes before she died. As the youngest of five children, Brian was born when Mom was 40 years old. At the time, the other four of us were nearly ready to launch off into college or apartments of our own, and so, for much of his childhood, Brian was almost like an only child. He and Mom had had a lot of quality time together and he was very close to her. I remember him once describing her as "my best friend."

My voice was gentle as I told him. He was obviously in shock, but said he was on his way. The call complete, I made my way down the hall, back to Mom.

The aides had laid her on her bed and sweetly arranged her so that she would look nice when I came back in to see her. I started to say goodbye and then realized I needed to do one more thing first. I rushed outside the door and ran up and down the halls, frantically searching until I found the nurse. I asked her to please, please not call the funeral home yet. I knew from experience with Dad that they come rather quickly, and I wanted Brian and I to have ample time to say goodbye before they came and took her away. The nurse agreed to wait and, relieved, I went back to the room to begin the sad task of saying goodbye to my dear mama.

First I stood at her head and stroked her hair over and over. It had been one of Mom's greatest simple pleasures when I did that. She would practically purr with the sensuous pleasure of having my fingers lightly caress her scalp.

I knew, of course, that Mom couldn't feel my touch. But a part of me sensed that she knew what I was doing; that she was watching and feeling my love as she beamed me her own.

I began murmuring to her, thanking her for her life and for being such a wonderful, loving mother. After a few minutes I started lightly stroking her arms and her hands. I found myself thanking her for all the times she had held us, all the times she had comforted us, all the thousands of meals she had cooked with those arms and hands.

Spontaneously I began doing a ritual of gratitude, thanking her for the breasts, now flaccid with age, that had once given me succor; and the belly that had once sheltered me in her womb. I just touched her and held her hands, thanking her over and over.

About this time both the aides came in to offer their solace. When one visits her parent every single day, one begins to know the regular aides quite well. I really liked and respected Mary and Nellie. They were both African American women, both grandmothers. Mary was tall, robust, and regal in her bearing; Nellie was petite and sweet. Together they enfolded me in their arms in a great threeway embrace, and like good mothers everywhere, they rocked me and whispered prayers and sweet words of comfort.

Over and over again I find that compassionate touch can release tears like nothing else. As I felt the sincere love and concern of these two dear women, I dissolved into the sobs I hadn't yet let myself express. Even though it was about 9 p.m. and I knew most of the residents were sound asleep, I started to bawl, howling with grief for the woman who had given me birth.

Losing your mother is such a sad rite of passage. But I was very blessed. I came from a home that was filled with love.

What a great blessing--to have been there when Mom drew her last breath, to have had sacred time alone with her, and then to be held by those two powerful yet tender women as I cried.
I am honored to have been the firstborn daughter of a soul like Barbara Ann Hendricks Greb.

Bless her forever and ever. Amen.

The Cat and the Buddhist Blessing

February 2017

I met Linda in early 2017. Her friend had seen my name on the care.com website and had called to see if I would be willing to meet Linda and, if Linda was agreeable, help her clean and organize her home a bit.

I had been told that Linda's adult daughter had passed just a couple weeks prior. Not only had her daughter been her only child, they had also shared Linda's small home and, together, had been administrators of a Tibetan Buddhist sangha[21] in the Mt. Shasta area of California. By all counts, they had been extremely close.

Linda must have been grieving greatly, but she hid it behind the most radiant smile. We liked one another immediately. I was told later that it was hard for her to trust people and that she was very private, but apparently I passed muster. We quickly became friends.

I had only been working for her part-time for a couple of weeks when Linda told me she needed me to go with her to the

---

[21] A sangha is a Buddhist community of monks, nuns, novices, and laity

doctor's. Linda was exceedingly nervous, worried that she wouldn't make it down the four steps outside her front door and into the van which I had pulled around to the front of the house. I didn't understand why she was so nervous.

When we got to the office, Linda explained that she'd been feeling very weak. The clinician asked Linda to walk down the hall so she could observe her. We were all surprised to see that Linda was so weak, she couldn't even stand up. At the point, the doctor decided to send her across the street to the emergency room.

Within a relatively short time, Linda was diagnosed with acute anemia. They soon discovered she would require not one, but two blood transfusions. Suddenly it occurred to me that I had never seen her anywhere but sitting on the chair behind her desk. Until that morning, as she was valiantly attempting to get into her van, I had never seen her take one single step anywhere. She had mentioned a couple times that she felt extremely weak, but none of us had had any clue just how incapicitated she had become.

My respect for her grew exponentially as I realized that even making it to that desk chair each morning from her bedroom down the short hall must have been an act of extreme will on her part. Taking her little dog to be tied outside to the porch rail didn't mean she was too lazy to take him for a walk, it meant she couldn't make it down the steps. And now I realized why she was so hungry and thirsty all the time. She, literally, did not have the energy to walk back and forth to the kitchen, let alone stand to prepare a meal or clean up afterwards. Now I also finally understood why her home was so messy. She couldn't do the dishes, couldn't put things away, couldn't take out the trash. It's a miracle she had never fallen.

On the way to the doctor's office that morning she had decided to get a coffee from the McDonald's drive-through. I persuaded her to get a breakfast sandwich, too. She was in heaven while rapturously eating her humble sandwich. Now I finally understood why it was such a thrill for her.

Linda rallied a bit after her transfusions but still needed hospital care. One afternoon a couple days later I was sitting with Linda when her smile disappeared. It was obvious to me that she was in discomfort because I had never seen her without that smile. I reported my concerns to the nurse more than once. The nurse replied that Linda was "just tired." Finally, after I had gone yet another time to the nurse's station to express my worries, a breathing treatment was ordered for Linda.

After this treatment Linda lapsed into sleep. I still wasn't completely assured she was okay, but I had her little dog to tend to. He was outside waiting for me in my cold car. Feeling torn, I left the hospital to take her little Scottie for a walk and then home for the night.

Early the next morning I got a call from Gaylen, one of Linda's closest friends. (Linda's three closest friends, all members of her Buddhist sangha, all lived out of state. I was taking care of details on their behalf.) The hospital had called Gaylen to say that Linda had gone downhill overnight. My heart rose to my throat. I hurried to take the dog on a walk and then get over to the hospital.

Linda didn't look good; she was unresponsive at this point. Meanwhile, Gaylen had begun calling various members of the local Buddhist community to come and do some chanting at Linda's bedside. By early afternoon, four of us were gathered around Linda, meditating, chanting and singing sacred prayers. It was in this sweet context that Linda took her last breath.

I was standing at her bedside when my cell phone rang. I was embarrassed that I hadn't turned off my phone. I quickly answered it, and thank God I did because it turned out to be Linda's teacher's nephew, a rinpoche[22] located in Boulder, Colorado. This nephew had received a call from one of Linda's friends informing him that her passing was imminent.

The timing of his call was perfect. He instructed me to lay my phone next to Linda's ear, and then he proceeded to chant the words that would assist her spirit into the afterlife.

After about ten minutes of chanting, he said goodbye and hung up. Linda's friends then arranged Linda's body in a position judged to be optimal for death and rebirth. I fussed with her hair

---

[22] A highly respected Buddhist teacher (pronouced rin'-poh-shay)

and the pendant she wore around her neck. And then we all said our goodbyes.

The funeral home arrived and Linda's body was gently and respectfully moved onto a gurney. One woman and I decided to accompany Linda down the hall and outside into the hearse. As the man was sliding her body into the back of the vehicle, I caught a glimpse of a gorgeous black cat sitting there by the side of the hearse. It felt rather unusual to see a cat out in the middle of a parking lot, with cars coming and going. I turned to Marie and said,"I think he came to say goodbye." At that he turned his head, looked at me, and blinked his beautiful eyes. Marie got goosebumps. Apparently, a woman who was a prime mover and shaker of the local Buddhist community had lost her cat just a couple of weeks before Linda had lost her beloved daughter. We all think the cat really did come to say goodbye.

There are events that happen in the physical world, and there are events that happen in the spiritual world. Those who knew Linda and her teacher Khempo believe he was orchestrating and guiding Linda's whole dying process from the other side. They would soon all be together once again—Linda, her daughter, and their teacher. They would continue their work and evolution in the world beyond this one.

All was in divine order.

Grief Is[23]

November 4, 2016

A year ago today my beautiful niece left this world. Although doctors tried valiantly to save her, they couldn't hold her; her soul had seen the Light of the next world and was ready to fly free. As she traveled toward the Light and was embraced by it, the Light became brighter still. And our world suddenly became dimmer.

Over the course of the last year, whenever I thought of Trisha I would feel such pain for my sister and her husband. What unbearable sorrow to lose one's only child. This morning as I sat with the awareness of her passing, the tears continued to flow long past what I had expected. It finally dawned on me: I didn't ache only for them, I ached for *myself*. I missed her, too. It didn't matter that I knew she was in a better place. I couldn't "think away" the grief. The heart feels what the heart feels.

After an hour or more of silently falling tears, I finally allowed myself to just bawl. Why contain all this grief in a tight little box? It was a relief to let the dam burst.

---

[23] https://www.cynthiagreb.com/grief/

In Burkina Faso in West Africa, they believe expressing great grief for the dead is absolutely essential. Unlike in America, there it is extremely taboo *not* to cry. Their funerals are an elaborate ritual in which the tears and wailing are actively cultivated and then released—for *all* the losses, *all* the grief, *all* the individual and collective pain. Malidoma Some tells us in his book *Of Water and the Spirit,* "Only by passionate expression can loss be tamed and assimilated into a form one can live with."

How much healthier it must be to have grief so sanctioned. I can only imagine how our bodies must suffer as we submerge our pain so deeply, afraid of letting anyone else see it. Why should we be ashamed of the grief that bears testimony to the love that we feel? Why should we hide the very thing that makes us most human?

With the passing of my parents and Trisha, my clients, uncles and boyfriends, I had recently become rather too well acquainted with death. But familiarity with death didn't mean I could escape the feelings that went along with it.

My friend Carol lost her beloved husband a few years ago to advanced Parkinson's disease. This once tall, good-looking, extremely intelligent and interesting man had become bed-bound, his body curved and small as his muscles continually contracted. After he died and dear ones were bathing his body, Carol told me he looked for all the world like an emaciated Christ.

Carol still actively grieves. She still wears black. She still reads about grief. She still writes about grief. She still aches each and every day. She marks every single anniversary--their first date, when they married, when he was diagnosed, when he first fell and went into the hospital, when he was born, when he died.

I visit Carol from time to time. Our visits are often three hours long; we always have so much to say. She is relieved to have someone with whom she can speak freely. She says people are often uncomfortable when she talks about David. The unspoken words are: "Get over it." But how does one get over the loss of a person who was omnipresent in every aspect of one's life? How does one act as if everything is normal when one's great love lies buried in a box in the ground?

Likewise, how does my sister get over the loss of her only beloved daughter? They shopped together, they picked up take-out together, they talked about Trisha's struggles with school, her dreams for the future, her love for her boyfriend. Seeing my sister and niece together, I often thought they were almost more like girlfriends or sisters than mother and daughter.

And how does my brother-in-law get over losing his precious little girl? He is physically disabled and almost always at home. The highlight of every day was when his sunshiny daughter returned home from school and they could talk about their days.

How does one cope with such a large hole in the fabric of one's life? How does one continue to embrace life when the one who was most lovingly embraced is no longer around?

Grief is. There are no tidy loose ends to tie up. It lingers and lingers and lingers. The heart feels what the heart feels. The mind can sometimes take control and say, "Okay, let's get on with life," but then--often when we least expect it--the heart will roar "NO! I will be heard!" And the tears flow yet again.

One thing is certain, where there is grief, you can be sure there was Love. As some wise person once said, "Grief is not a sign of weakness, nor a lack of faith... It is the price of love."

P.S. Here is the Grace part of this story. As I was remembering Trisha and tears were sliding continuously down my face, I plucked a paper towel from the counter in order to blot my eyes. I was astonished to notice that my tears had left a perfect heart shaped drop of moisture on the towel. I absolutely *know* Trisha orchestrated that. I know she was was telling me she loved me.

Grace.

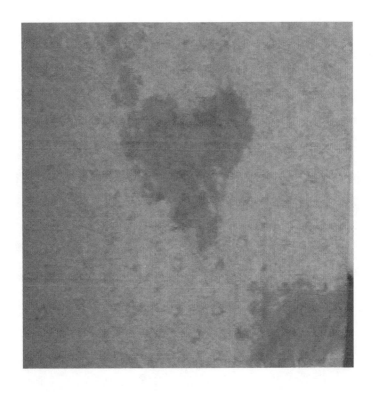

Perfect heart on paper towel after I blotted my tears.

Dreams of Our Loved Ones on the Other Side[24]

May 4, 2016

This afternoon I went into the bank and my favorite teller greeted me by name. "What are you doing this weekend?" she asked cheerfully.

I replied, "I'm giving a talk on *Death, Dreams, and the Afterlife.*"

There was no response. I thought maybe she had some judgments about the title or theme of my talk. But then I heard her quietly ask, "Do you mean dreams from someone we love?"

I nodded yes. Then it suddenly dawned on me. "Have you had a dream like this?" I asked.

She nodded.

I probed, "Was it like a visitation?"

"Yes," she told me. "It felt really real."

I asked softly, "Can you tell me who it was about?"

"My father," she replied, tears instantly springing to her eyes.

---

[24] https://www.cynthiagreb.com/dreams-from-our-deceased-loved-ones/

Such is the power of dreams from those who love us.

I use the word "from" very intentionally. I believe many of those who leave this plane of existence are very much looking for ways to communicate with those of us left behind. Most of us have yet to learn how to be open to messages from our deceased loved ones, but fortunately sometimes they can "sneak in" a visit while we're dreaming. In waking reality, we might unintentionally put up the barriers of non-belief. For instance, if we think of our loved one and the sun comes suddenly bursting through the clouds, or a meaningful song suddenly plays on the radio, we might write these messages off as "just a coincidence." However, when we dream, our defenses are down because our logical mind is turned off. It's a great way for them to communicate with us.

Some of you who are mourning the death of a loved one may be asking yourself right now, *'Why haven't I had such a dream?'* Sadly, when our grief is too raw, apparently it somehow seems to block communication. That is why sometimes a neighbor or a more distant relation may have dreams of your loved one whereas you have not (yet). It seems to have to do with the vibration. When we are really sad or depressed, our vibration is lower. On the other hand, those in the realm of spirit have a higher vibration, and it is often more difficult for them to access us when there is a mismatch of frequency. Fortunately, as we begin to heal and allow peace and joy back into our lives, this can change.

I have had a few notable dreams of people I know who are "on the other side." For instance, a couple years ago, John, a neighbor in the **village** where I grew up, died of cancer. A few days later he appeared to me in a dream. There was no plot, he just seemed to want to show me that he was "alive" and quite healthy and happy.

Another particularly memorable dream was about Danny. Danny was a high school classmate who occasionally attended my church. I was stunned when I learned he had died in a fiery car crash. At the funeral, his sister told me he'd always wanted to ask me out but could never quite get up the courage. Sometime later I dreamed I was crawling on my hands and knees through a hallway that was getting progressively tighter. At one point the hallway veered to the right. As I turned the corner, there before me "filling the screen" of my dream was Danny's face, huge and shining so bright I could scarcely look at him. It brought to mind stories of near-death experiences and how the souls go through a tunnel. Danny was clearly through the tunnel and being reborn into a new life. He was absolutely radiant and whole!

A few years ago I dreamed of my paternal grandmother, with whom I had been especially close. In the dream I was riding in a bus when I heard a few crystal clear lovely chimes. (Only a few times have I ever heard chimes in my dreams. In every case they signaled something very significant and special was about to happen.) I found myself turning around, and there in the seat behind me was my wonderful grandmother. She looked pretty and "shiny," healthier and rosier than I had ever seen her. She just beamed me this brilliant smile. And although I would have loved to have received a message, that beautiful image of her shining loving face was quite enough.

I think sometimes they just want to show us that they are fully alive and happy. They want us to know they haven't forgotten us and they still love us.

I once shared a dream on Facebook in which I had died, but there was no drama around it; it was just a fact. I was with others whom I knew had also died. We were all casually walking around together. We weren't like ghosts, we were all perfectly fine and healthy just like in "regular life."

As usual on Facebook, friends responded with comments. One woman shared about her cousin who had been completely devastated after his mother died. He just couldn't seem to get over it. He so badly wanted to hear from her. Finally he had the following dream:

> He was in a diner. Every booth was packed. People were sitting, crammed shoulder to shoulder. Across from each person was a loved one--a loved one who had passsed. And each one of them was saying, "I am okay. I love you so much. I have to go now."

We are often so afraid of death, and when our loved ones die, we are so bereft. But I imagine if they had one thing they could tell us, it would be this: "Don't worry. I love you. I'm alive and well.

There is no death where we are. Life continues, it's just in a different form."

Joshua trees at sunset

An Angel Gets His Wings

March 2014

The way death works in this country, there is little time to sit with our feelings of grief because most of us are bombarded with decisions about the funeral, the casket, the cemetery, the flowers, a memorial service, food following the service, getting death certificates, notifying friends and family, etc. It's an exhausting time. But for some people this is a blessing because it provides a buffer so that the feelings don't come crashing in all at once.

After Dad's death, I buried myself in the details of planning the memorial service and funeral. My siblings took care of all the rest, thank goodness. We had the burial first, with only close family and a couple friends; the memorial service was the following day and was attended by over two hundred people. Then afterwards, with barely a breath, I threw myself into helping sort through, sell, give away, store, and toss the decades of things that had accumulated in the family home. Because of the reverse mortgage we'd obtained in order to afford Mom and Dad's caregivers (after I burned out caring for them myself), the house would soon be going to the bank. I, in turn, would be returning to my home in Colorado. Even though I was exhausted, I pushed myself to do this work before I left because I very much wanted to spare my brother the headache of dealing with it himself. He had already done so much over the years while my one sister and I lived out of state.

I was so stressed and sad. Most days I don't think I even bathed. I seldom left the house. It was just nose to the grindstone. In retrospect, it was ridiculously unwise and unkind to my grieving self to dive into this enormous task so soon. It was way too much pressure.

Another reason I was pushing myself so hard was because I had been given a scholarship to a wonderful workshop in California. The timing was obviously very, very bad because I was still in the throes of grief. But the theme of this workshop was very important to me[25], and a scholarship was a rare and lovely gift. As I was debating whether or not to go, I finally acknowledged I couldn't deny the appeal of just getting away after all the months of sorrow and responsibility. And so, I went.

My dear friend Henry picked me up at LAX. He and his wife kindly allowed me to stay at their home a couple of days. But no sooner had I arrived than I got sick--like, food poisoning sick. I am seldom ill. My friends thought it was a natural response to the pressure and the grief. Fortunately I recovered after one day,

---

[25] "Medicine for the Earth and Healing with Spiritual Light," by Sandra Ingerman. This powerful workshop teaches how we can effect change at an environmental level with the power of our intention and our focus on love. Sandra writes about this beautifully here: http://www.sandraingerman.com/medicinefortheearth.html

and Henry generously drove me down to Joshua Tree where the workshop was to be.

While I was at lunch one day sitting with a couple of workshop participants, I asked, "What is it you love to do?" (Don't you think this is an infinitely more interesting question than "What do you do for a living?") This lovely man named Tahir replied that he loved to do psychopomp work. Most people--even educated people--have never heard of that word. However, those acquainted with shamanism have sometimes heard of it. I was first exposed to the word over a decade before when, shortly after 9/11, a Native American woman guided our ministry class in the psychopomp work of guiding into the Light the lost and bewildered souls of the Trade Towers disaster.

After Tahir told me about his passion, I confessed that my father had died just three weeks before. Tahir graciously asked if I wanted him to check in with my father. I realized that I had been surprised that after all the many hundreds of hours I had spent with Dad in his final months, I hadn't felt his spirit around me following his death. So gratefully, and with tears pooling in my eyes, I nodded and said that yes, I'd like that very much.

Several hours later, when we were all gathering for the evening session, Tahir found me. He told me he'd seen my father. He said Dad had been waiting because he was worried about me. Then he gave me Dad's message. It was summed up in the following words: "Find your community. And do what you love."

While our teacher began her teaching that evening, silent tears slid down my face. They continued to flow for about forty minutes. I was simultaneously thrilled to have heard from Dad, and extremely sad that he'd waited to move on because of me. After all the physical and emotional discomfort and trauma of his last few months, the very last thing I wanted was to delay Dad's return to heaven!

After the evening session was over, I slowly made my way to my tent. Because I hadn't been making any money while I was spending time with both Dad and Mom, I couldn't afford to have indoor lodging. So I was camping on the premises at the outer edge of the conference center, in an unlit place far away from the dorms, the cafeteria, and the hall where we met each day. It was dark and I used my flashlight to carefully pick my way over the desert terrain toward my tent, my haven for the night.

I was extremely grateful to finally have some time to myself.

Once inside the tent I puttered a bit, tidying up my clothes and clutter. In my suitcase, I discovered the wind chimes I'd brought with me at the suggestion of a wise friend. She had suggested to me that I hang them after my father died because he might use them to communicate with me. I hadn't thought to hang them before, but now suddenly it felt like a good time. I hung them from the crossed bars at the top of the domed part of my tent and then laid down to slip into some much needed slumber.

About 3:00 a.m., I heard two footsteps outside my tent. Just two. I was alarmed. I was a woman all alone in a dark and remote area. There were a couple of tents in the general vicinity, but none were close by me. Then I remembered an incident that had happened about twelve or thirteen years earlier when I went on my first vision quest. During one of those three nights, I had distinctly heard two steps on the hill behind me where I sat in the woods. Later, my teacher told me those steps had been made by a spirit. At the time, that had been a new concept (and experience) for me, but by the time I'd arrived in Joshua Tree, it seemed perfectly plausible. Thinking maybe the same thing was true this time, and feeling way too exhausted to stay awake worrying about it, I laid back down in my sleeping bag.

Within moments, my chimes started to ring. And they didn't stop! They rang and rang and rang and rang! And then the tent started billowing with a wind that Tahir later told me he didn't remember happening. Those chimes swayed and clanged and rang and rang. And the whole time this was going on I was laying there with a big grin on my face, absolutely and unequivocally sure that it was Dad telling me he'd moved on.

Those chimes rang for a full hour.

I couldn't help but think of the movie *It's a Wonderful Life* when the little girl tells her father, played by Jimmy Stewart, "My teacher says that every time a bell rings, an angel gets its wings."

Well done, Dad! Happy Graduation!

Epilogue

December 2018

At the time of this writing, three years have passed since that unexpected spate of deaths and loss in my life. I've noticed that the feeling of loss shifts and changes over time.

I found that after each of my parents passed, I needed a few months to restore myself. A lot had happened in the months prior to each death; there was a lot to absorb, process, and recover from. However, I am pleased to report that, for me, the "missing them" phenomenon was not as pronounced a factor as I had anticipated. Partly it was because I could feel their spirit around me. When I thought of them, at some level, I could feel them nearby. I sensed they were still with me.

I'm guessing this phenomenon does not apply to all who grieve. For some it will be unspeakably hard for a very long time time. The loss of a beloved child or spouse, for instance, is likely to be infinitely more difficult than the loss of parents who have lived a long life. However, when we understand at a deeper level that there is no "end" but only a transition from one form to another, it can make a big difference in the grieving process. Likewise, perhaps we can find great comfort when we realize that Love never ever ends. Death is no match for love. Love is eternal.

For both those who believe in God and an afterlife (as well as those who don't), I highly recommend reading books about "near-death" experiences. (This term, by the way, is not really accurate. These people were not *near* death; they were declared clinically dead![26] And then they "came back." It might be more accurate to call these "resurrection experiences!") I find resurrection stories extremely inspiring. It can help so much to hear that there is a world of ineffable love and peace on "the other side." [27]

I believe that my own strong belief in life after death, absolutely confirmed by powerful stories of the millions (!) of people who have come back from a visit there, lessened my grief considerably.[28] How can I remain sad when those I love are in a place without war, hatred, hunger, or sickness? How can I weep when they are immersed in an ocean of love? Yes, I may miss them, of course, but I know that they are okay--*more* than okay. It doesn't serve me to clutch and cling to sorrow. And certainly my loved ones wouldn't want me to mourn forever, constantly

---

[26] I first read thoughts about this misnomer in Judy Bachrach's wonderful book, *Glimpsing Heaven: The Stories and Science of Life after Death*. She suggests calling them "death travelers"--people who explore a world the rest of us don't have access to.

[27] Interestingly, many different sources report that near-death experiences happen to both those who believe in God and an afterlife and those who don't!

[28] https://www.theepochtimes.com/how-common-are-near-death-experiences-ndes-by-the-numbers_757401.html

putting my life on hold. Grief will certainly bubble up to the surface at various times, but perhaps we can eventually learn to let it flow through us, not take up permanent residence.

I want to refer briefly to another kind of grief. When my husband and I separated, I was feeling a huge mixture of emotions. Primarily I was sad, certainly. We'd been together nine years and he was a very good man. Secondly, I felt shame and guilt. Mine would be the first, and possibly only, divorce in my immediate family. And I certainly didn't want to cause pain to my husband or stepson. Thirdly, I confess I felt a bit of excitement to be single again and living alone, with all the freedom that implies. But the predominant emotion was sadness.

Because of the shame and guilt, I was reluctant to let anyone see any hint of happiness in me. At a subconscious level, I thought that people would think I didn't love my husband or that I wasn't a good person if I didn't wallow in sadness as I mourned the end of our relationship.

Then one day, about three months after our separation, my husband (who had begun seeing someone else) wisely counseled me to, "Let the joy in." Having that permission made a huge difference in my life. In fact, it was a turning point for me.

If you are grieving, perhaps you, too, can allow yourself to let in little (or big) moments of joy. Your loved one would certainly want that for you!

In this collection of stories and essays that you have just read, I allowed my very human self to be revealed. All of my messy emotions, all of my guilt and exhaustion, all my fallibilities, all of my unhealed wounds were on full display. Were I to go back in time and counsel my own self, I would have encouraged considerably more kindness to myself. I would have reminded myself, over and over, to fill my well first *before* I ventured out to be present for my parents or my clients.

I am convinced that I was presented with so many opportunities to be a caregiver for others because I had so many lessons to learn. Like many women, I was willing to dive in and do what needed to be done for those I love. But, like many, I had trouble taking care of myself in the process.

I hope that you will take my heartfelt advice and allow for significant self-care and respite during your caregiving days, months, or years. It is not easy work.

I believe we are on this planet to love, to learn, and to grow. So, what can we learn from these challenging times at the threshold of living and dying? And what can we do to make it a bit easier for everyone concerned?

- Love to the best of your ability.
- Try to be present in the moment.
- Remember also to love yourself in the midst of this great life passage.
- Be compassionate--to others *and* yourself.
- Take time to rest and fill your well.
- Feed your soul. Nourish your spirit.
- Ask for what you need.
- Take time to talk with friends, a therapist, or a clergyperson. This is a challenging time and you deserve someone to listen to you and be there for you.
- Remember to call on your angels, God, and guides for support.
- Pray for those who care for your loved one.
- Let go. You can't control this process.
- Remember that there are lessons for you in this journey.
- Remember that your loved one has lessons to learn as well.
- Trust that there is a divine plan.
- Breathe.

Right at the time I was attending to the final details of this book, I was exposed to the following very beautiful prayer. It is meant to be said following the death of a loved one. It is one of the more profound prayers I've ever seen.

Oh Thou
The cause and effect of the whole universe
The source from whence we have come
And the goal toward which we are bound
Receive this soul, _____, who is coming to Thee
Into Thy parental arms.
May Thy forgiving glance heal her heart.

Lift her from the denseness of the earth.
Surround her with the light of Thine own spirit.
Raise her up to heaven
Which is her true dwelling place.
We pray Thee, grant her the blessing
Of Thy most exalted presence.

May her life upon earth
Become as a dream to her waking soul.
And let her thirsting eyes behold
The glorious vision of Thy sunshine.

Amen.[29]

---

[29] Prayer by Hazrat Inayat Khan.

In this great journey of life, death, and rebirth, I wish you peace.

Of one thing I am very sure: whether on this side of the veil or the other, Love is present. May you be comforted by Love as you bask in its eternal presence.

Notes

Feel free to use these next few pages for thoughts and feelings that have arisen for you over the course of reading this book.

Acknowledgments and Gratitude

This book never would have happened had multiple extremely special people not chosen to leave this world. And so, first let me acknowledge these dear people and my lovely family:

To my beloved parents who not only gave me life, but beautifully raised me and my four siblings with ever so much love. Thank you forever and ever, Barbara and Norman Greb. I know we will be connected throughout eternity.

To the four grandparents who gave my parents life, and to Grandmom Lear, the great aunt who raised my mother from the time she was one year old. Thank you: Hilda Lear, Anna and Lester Hendricks, Harry Greb, and an extra special thank you to Doris Christiana Greb. (I strongly suspect she's one of my guardian angels.) I love you all.

To my four amazing siblings and their spouses and girlfriends. Thank you for all that you do and all that you are. I couldn't ask for better sisters and brothers. (According to birth order): To Eric, for being such a man of integrity and for being such a phenomenal father to your kids as well as grandfather to your grandchildren; to Karen, for being endlessly compassionate, generous, and kind to all of your family, your patients, and everyone you meet. (Everyone who knows you thinks you are a very special nurse); to Janice, for being so smart and capable and good-hearted, and such a wonderful wife and mother; and to Brian, for being so interesting and authentic, talented and kind-hearted. And an extra special thank you to my sister-in-law Colette for selflessly giving so much time, love, and energy to my parents in their later years, and for being so knowledgeable and diligent, and for being a sisterfriend.

To my beloved niece Trisha. Everyone who knew you loved you, Trisha. You were and are an incredibly bright light, full of great love, goodness, and joy. You are dearly missed by so many.

To my dear uncles. Thank you, Uncle Harry, for all your love; Uncle Bill for all your positivity; and Uncle Paul for your great smile and laughter.

To my boyfriends. Thank you, Rudy Schulz, for letting me be a part of your life for a while and for communicating with me after you passed. Thank you, Dan Haverkamp, for being such an extraordinary human being, so talented and good-hearted. I was truly blessed to have known you. And thank you, Ron Fluck, for being such a great guy and good friend.

Next, thank you most profoundly to those friends and family members who opened their homes to me and were so generous with their emotional support and love during the challenging times caring for my parents:
- First and foremost, to Philip and Helene who so kindly put up with me for so long even when they were so stressed

running their store during the busy holiday months. Thank you so much, you two, for so generously giving me a safe haven as I was going through so many struggles. Thank you for sharing your incredibly special, wonderful, and sweet dogs, for sharing your food, and even lending me your car! You have earned so many brownie points for your exceptional kindness. I will never be able to repay you. I am grateful beyond measure. You are exceptional people.

- Secondly, to my dear friend Karen, who went above and beyond giving me a place to find my feet as I returned to Santa Fe, and then again after I broke my ankle just three months later. Thank you, Karen, for giving me a place to heal and to write. You are a beautiful and generous soul. May your kindness be returned a thousandfold.

- To Scott and Melissa for welcoming me into your home to care for your beloved animals and for giving me sanctuary. What a haven you have created!

- To Colette and Eric for always welcoming me into your beautiful home and hearts. You loved me (and fed me) through it all.

- To Connie for always being so gracious and kind. Thank you for sharing your serene home, your car, and your dear self.

- To Mike and Judy for giving me a place to stay when I was at my wit's end.

- To Betsy for being such an incredible friend as well as an extraordinary healer, wise woman, and soul sister. Thank you for being such an enormous support to me. I am so grateful for you!

- To Mike for always being there for me. I don't know what I would have done without you. Truly. You are such an incredible gift.
- To George T. for always believing in me and my purpose and potential. And for being such an extraordinary soul. (I hope you realize that someday!)
- To Barbara and Phil for a home and kindness and friendship. And for making the world a better place!
- To Durwood for giving me respite when I needed it most.
- To Edie for understanding how sad it is to lose great parents.

To all of the hospice patients who provided me with an opportunity to deepen in compassion, and **to all the staff I was so very privileged to work with.**

To my caregiving clients and their families for so many blessings and lessons. David, for having so much dignity and patience even in the face of such a debilitating disease--I wish I had known you longer; Vera, for being such a good soul; Mary, for being such a talented woman with such a huge spirit--thank you for being my friend; Helen, for the incredible dream; and others whose names have fled my memory, but not your faces, spirit, nor great courage. Thank you, too, especially to Carol, for being such an extraordinarily loving wife to David and for modeling conscious grief so powerfully; to Dr. Vince Palermo, for being such a dedicated beloved to his Mary and for continuing to be such a dear friend; and to Kirsten, for being... you!

To those dear friends who read this book, I thank you so very much. Bless you, bless you, bless you for being so generous with your time and wonderful suggestions. Thank you, dear Amara, Betsy, Lady, Patti, and Robin for reading the first drafts. You are such dear friends and I love and respect you so much. And thank you so much, Lea, for so graciously reading the second edition. I am so grateful!

To my generous and irreplaceable tech support friends. Mike, I would be helpless without you. Thank you so, so, so much for "saving" me over and over again! Someday I'll be able to pay you what you're worth! Thank you also, dear Andree, and Dianne, too.

And last on this list but at the very top of my heart and soul, **thank you to the great Mother/Father God who is ever present with a Love more vast than we can ever begin to imagine on this side of the veil. I owe You everything.**

May the words on these pages touch the hearts of every reader. May your tender and beautiful souls be filled with great Grace as you navigate the remaining days of your life on this dear planet. Remember, we are Loved!

With love and gratitude,
Cynthia

Bibliography

Alexander, Eben, M.D. *Proof of Heaven: A Neurosurgeon's Journey into the Afterlife.* **New York: Simon and Schuster, 2012.**

This popular book chronicles the spiritual journey of a topnotch neurosurgeon who, after an especially virulent infection, finds himself in a week-long coma from which he was not expected to recover. During this time he experienced unfathomable worlds beyond the physical plane. He was astounded to realize his consciousness was present and aware even as his physical brain had clearly ceased to function. Like many people who've had a glimpse of life on the other side, he struggled to put into words the palpable yet absolutely ineffable love he felt in these other realms. His life was forever changed as a result of this experience.

Bachrach, Judy. *Glimpsing Heaven: The Stories and Science of Life after Death.* **Washington, D.C.: The National Geographic Association, 2014.**

The death of someone very dear to this journalist impels her to dive into exhaustive research about the subject of life after death. She conducts scores of interviews with people who have died and returned to tell their tales. She calls them "death travelers." She also interviews nurses, doctors, and scientists. This is a superb book and a comprehensive exploration of what happens after people die.

Callanan, Maggie and Patricia Kelley. *Final Gifts: Understanding the Special Awareness, Needs, and Communications of the Dying.* New York: Simon & Schuster, 2012.

This classic book by former hospice nurses reveals the many ways that those nearing the end of life communicate their thoughts and feelings. This is an extremely wise and compassionate guide, teaching us how to respectfully and gracefully assist the dying in having their emotional and spiritual needs met.

Kagan, Annie. *The Afterlife of Billy Fingers: How My Bad-Boy Brother Proved to Me There's Life After Death.* Charlottesville, Virginia: Hampton Roads Publishing Company, Inc., 2013.

This fascinating book reads like fiction but is a true account of a woman struggling with the unexpected death of her beloved but estranged often-troubled brother. Like most of us who grieve, the author is extremely despondent for a while, but then during periods of meditation she begins to hear his voice. At first reluctant to believe what she is hearing, eventually she receives enough proof that she begins to not just believe, but eagerly anticipate these joyous revelations from the afterlife. What sets this book apart is 1) its wonderful readability, and 2) unlike other books in the life-after-death genre, her brother continues to report about the afterlife for about a year after his passing. I found particularly captivating the part in which his soul has merged so deeply into the great Oneness of everything that he has trouble "reconstituting himself" enough to form the words to convey to her what he is experiencing. But fortunately for us, he knows his experience is important for earthbound folks to know.

I found both his and her story riveting and beyond profound. It is a book I recommend to others often.

Kahn, Leslie. *Surviving Death: A Journalist Investigates Evidence for an Afterlife.* New York: Crown Archetype, 2017.

If you are someone who needs proof about whether or not there is a life beyond this physical world that we know, Kahn conducts exhaustive research on the topic. There are many fascinating case studies.

Kerr, Patti. *I Love You, Who Are You? Loving and Caring for a Patient with Alzheimer's.* 2nd ed. Flemington, New Jersey: Along the Way Press, 2019.

This book is a compassionate and comprehensive guide for anyone who loves or cares for someone with Alzheimer's. The author shares her own experiences caring for her mother, as well as stories gleaned from scores of interviews with other stressed-out caregivers. This book is a beautiful compilation of resources and advice. The author is extremely knowledgeable on this subject. I truly wish I had had this book before my father started his decline.

Kubler-Ross, Elizabeth. *On Death and Dying: What the Dying Have to Teach Doctors, Nurses, Clergy and Their Own Families.* **New York: Macmillan Publishing Company, 1969.**

This is the seminal book in which Kubler-Ross, a medical doctor, psychiatrist, and expert on death, explored the five stages that are traversed by those facing the end of their lives (denial, anger, bargaining, depression, acceptance.) She advocated treating terminal patients with respect--as human beings with manifold needs and desires who deserve to be included in the discussion about their care, as well as given the opportunity to share their feelings about approaching the end of life. These were considered rather radical ideas at the time.

Moody, Raymond A., Jr., M.D. *Life after Life: The Bestselling Original Investigation that Revealed "Near-Death" Experiences.* **3rd ed. New York: HarperCollins Publishers, 2015.**

In this classic, Moody gathers testimonies from more than 100 people who experienced clinical death, were resuscitated, and had amazing stories to tell about their time beyond the physical plane.

Moss, Robert. *The Dreamer's Book of the Dead: A Soul Traveler's Guide to Death, Dying, and the Other Side.* Rochester, Vermont: Destiny Books, 2005.

This book if for those who readily understand that there are multiple worlds and dimensions, and that all the many realities are much more magical and mystical than we have been taught. Moss, a powerful dream teacher, is a true shaman though he would never call himself that. (No real shaman would ever define him or herself as such.) Moss receives much teaching in his dreams and graciously shares his knowledge. In *Dreamer's Book of the Dead* some impressive clues are given about what happens in the afterlife.

Rodegast, Pat and Judith Stanton. *Emmanuel's Book: A Manual for Living Comfortably in the Cosmos.* New York: Bantam Books, 1987.

I loved this book when I first encountered it years ago and, having remembered a delightful and wise section about death, I found Emmanuel once again. Because its truths are eternal, this book holds up very well over time. It is a joy to read. This book is where I first remember reading about death being such a relief and release for the soul. Leaving the body is, as he says, "like taking off a tight shoe."[30]

Some, Malidoma Patrice. *Of Water and the Spirit: Ritual, Magic and Initiation in the Life of an African Shaman.* New York: the Penguin Group, 1994.

This is an absolutely fascinating book about a man who, as a young child, was kidnapped from his traditional African village and placed in a rigid Catholic boarding school a thousand miles away. When, as a teenager, he makes his escape and miraculously finds his way home, the elders decide he must first go through a powerful rite of initiation if he is to remain.

There is a beautiful section in the early part of the book which describes at length the three-day funeral of his well-respected and beloved medicine man grandfather. Western people have much to learn about the power and importance of expressing our grief.

Smartt, Lisa. *Words at the Threshold: What We Say as We're Nearing Death.* Novato, California: New World Library, 2017.

---

[30] *Emmanuel's Book*, compiled by Pat Rodegast an Judith Stanton, p. 169

The author had the privilege of studying with Dr. Raymond Moody, who wrote the groundbreaking book *Life After Life*. In her work with him Smartt founded the Final Words Project, in which abundant research was conducted, studying the language of those who were nearing death.

Cynthia Greb is a writer, artist, former hospice chaplain, and frequent caregiver of humans and animals.

To learn more, or to schedule talks, workshops, in-services, or retreats, visit www.cynthiagreb.com.

Made in the USA
Middletown, DE
26 August 2021